CONCILIUM

Religion in the Seventies

CONCILIUM

New Series: Volume 6, Number 9: Encounter

HUMANISM AND CHRISTIANITY

Edited by
Claude Geffré

Herder and Herder

1973
HERDER AND HERDER NEW YORK
815 Second Avenue
New York 10017

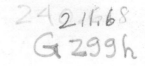
ISBN: 0–8164–2542–6

Cum approbatione Ecclesiastica

Library of Congress Catalog Card Number: 72–12424

Printed in the United States

CONTENTS

PART II
BULLETIN

Editorial

The Crisis of Humanism and the Future of Theology

IN SO FAR as theologians aim to remain faithful to the Word of God today, their task is always new. The theology is a creative renewal of the Christian message in the service of man and the questions he asks. It is the sphere within which dialogue takes place between Christianity and society. It is clear from the whole history of theology that what is often taken for a confrontation between the Christian message *per se* and a changed society is in many cases only a conflict between an historically conditioned expression of Christianity and that society. Theologians are therefore led by society itself to question critically the traditional structures of theology brought about by the encounter between faith and human thought. In this number of *Concilium*, the reverse takes place—mindful of our theological responsibilities, we propose to reflect about the social change caused by the "crisis of humanism" in the West.

It is easy to ask ironically whether the "death of man" is no more than a fashionable slogan made popular by French intellectuals and to say that this contestation of humanism is simply a luxury enjoyed by the rich societies of the West. As all the contributors to this number show, we are confronted by a very important social change and one which Christian thinkers must take seriously if they are not to be once again too late in their response to its obvious ideological challenge, which is already known to them from the past. What they have to do is to understand the contestation of our past society so as to be able to contest the society of today with its totalitarian claims.

In the past, all atheistic and religious ideologies claimed to be based on "humanism", with the result that the very word is now viewed with suspicion. J.-M. Domenach has tried, for example, to disentangle the complex skein of literary, scientific, social and economic factors which have led to this decline in humanism, which coincided, paradoxically, with a great increase in the study and the importance of the humane sciences. The application of the linguistic model to the humane sciences has made the destruction of man, as a subject who makes himself in history, a methodological necessity. What is more, together with this formalism and this anti-humanism that characterizes so many aspects of the humane sciences, there is a strong tendency in contemporary philosophy to oppose subjectivity.

Bearing in mind the new interdisciplinary approach of *Concilium*, we have asked for contributions within their own fields from some notable representatives of the humane sciences, comparative religion and philosophy. Any examination of the social changes that are taking place in the world today is in a sense a theological undertaking, in so far as it is true that the history of a society, as the vehicle of a certain image of man and the world, is important for our understanding of the Word of God. Before going into the symptoms underlying this decline in humanism, however, it is valuable to state what is involved theologically in this investigation.

I. The Theological Task in a Reflection about Humanism

1. For about fifteen years now, theologians have said again and again that, although we have a "theology", we have no "anthropology". An attempt was made to correct this situation in the Constitution on the Church in the Modern World (*Gaudium et Spes*) and this was followed by a number of Christian anthropologies. One of the most important tasks of these Christian studies of man was to overcome the contestation of atheistic humanism and to restore their Christian integrity to many varieties of humanism which often contained laicized Christian values. Now, however, in their anxiety to take part in dialogue

with atheistic humanists, Christians may seriously ask themselves whether their thinking about man is not lagging behind that of the atheists, whose most meaningful contribution nowadays is in the sphere of anti-humanism. "Nihilistic formalism" and "structural anti-humanism" are terms that are frequently heard in connection with the structuralism of C. Lévi-Strauss, L. Althusser and M. Foucault. Has not man, Foucault has asked, "discovered that he is neither at the centre of creation, nor in the middle of space, not even at the summit or at the end of life?"

This new form of atheism criticizes both atheistic and Christian humanism. The death of God of necessity leads to the death of man as a bearer of meaning. Since the time of Feuerbach, atheistic humanism has been no more than an inverted religious system (see Y. Labbé's article on "Humanism and Religion"). As a result, the whole field of study has been changed in this new atheism and anthropology, humanism and ideology have been forsaken for the fringe areas of science. Christians who see themselves as the guardians of humanism should therefore ask serious questions about the ambiguity of this atheistic programme. Does the permanently present reality of the gospel message concerning man have to be made manifest or does a certain ideological conception of Western man have rather to be defended by making that conception sacral?

2. The convenient title "the end of humanism" may cover such very serious questions as the elimination of the word as a bearer of meaning, of man as a meaningful intentionality and of history as the history of man's freedom. To discredit humanism in this way involves the danger of a radical contestation with Christian theology, because the very possibility of revelation and of faith itself is called into question. If we keep to the principles of a structural approach, we shall be confined to pure arguments and shall have no hidden textual meanings to interpret. The meaning will be confused with the text in the mechanism of its production. Similarly, it is futile to try to interpret man's religious consciousness as a sign of transcendence. What has to be done is to produce its intelligible space from its unconscious and its socio-economic structures. This disappearance of man as a meaningful subject reduces to nothing the intelligible space from which the language of faith can still have meaning.

Confronted with this anti-humanism, Christians are tempted to retreat into pure fideism. Even though it may be true that theologians ought to be suspicious of emphasizing humanism, they cannot cease to insist on the anthropological presuppositions of Christian faith. Again, they can profitably make use of the structural method in theology, while contesting the ideology which often goes with structuralism. It is possible to "objectivize" man more and more from the biological, psychological and sociological points of view in the light of modern anthropology, yet at the same time not to reduce him as a spiritual destiny and as a being who responds to a Word which is not exhausted in its cultural mediations (see A. Ganoczy's article). In view of this tendency to reduce man on the part of the humane sciences, theologians are confronted with the task of making a clearer distinction between the various levels at which man's experience and his linguistic expression of that experience are to be interpreted and of showing how the adventure of meaning is articulated through the game of unconscious or conscious structures, which may be the object of scientific explanation.

3. It is remarkable that, precisely at a time when humanism is viewed with such suspicion, theologians are above all preoccupied with the task of bringing to light the anthropological meaning of the Word of God. Since Bultmann, the main hermeneutical task has been the demythologization of false objectivizations of the Word of God so as to retain only what concerns man in his interpretation of himself. But what is the man who is involved here? Is it not the man who no longer belongs to our social sphere? The theologies based on "Christianity without God" are the ultimate point in the development of this anthropological reduction of Christian thought, an atheistic hermeneutical understanding inaugurated by Feuerbach ("God is a word, the only meaning of which is man").

Paradoxically, the present contestation with humanism could be beneficial if it were to make theologians conscious of the fact that they have more to do than simply to compete with secular ideologies. Their essential task is to restate in the present situation what Christianity has inherited from revelation. Jesus Christ and Christian man will lose meaning if they are not discussed within the framework of their relationship with God. It is pos-

sible for fruitful dialogue to exist between the humane sciences
and Christian anthropology, but only on condition that the latter
does not lose its identity, its formal object and its conviction that
man is open to God in and through Jesus Christ.

In this context, the importance of the two strictly theological
contributions to this number (by A. Ganoczy and W. Pannenberg) cannot be overemphasized. In the light of its specific formal
object, Christian anthropology can still listen profitably to the
criticism made by modern "secular" anthropology of a theological tradition in which Christian man has too often been identified
with universal, natural man, in the Graeco-Roman tradition, or
with the classical figure of man in bourgeois ideology. Of course,
we are not so naïve as to pretend that there is no danger to Christian anthropology in the present crisis of humanism. But, while
an anti-humanism that is not in any sense required by the praxis
of the humane sciences *per se* has to be opposed, we have also to
be courageous enough to criticize the concepts of our own Christian anthropology.

4. Whatever its ideological causes may be, the crisis of humanism is also the result of a tragic human destiny throughout the
past twenty-five or so years. The present revolt among young
people against a certain image of man and the world is the consequence of an awareness of the contradiction that exists between
the values proclaimed by humanism and the inhuman conditions
of life imposed on so many millions of human beings. As
J.-M. Domenach has quoted in his article, "Before having the
idea of the death of man, our age lived it". Modern man remem-
bers death in the concentration camps and still witnesses genocide. He knows of the dangers which threaten man's future—
famine, poverty, pollution, and so on—and experiences the de-
humanizing restrictions imposed by an industrial society intent
on economic growth at any price. This dehumanization, even
destruction, of man is expressed in many ways in contemporary
art and literature.

In this situation, it is natural enough for the Church to want
to be the bulwark of humanism. In the past, however, it has too
often been allied to a kind of Western humanism which has
succeeded in concealing or justifying scandalously inhuman
situations. Today, the Church has, in the name of the Word en-

trusted to it, that is "man is made in the image and likeness of God", to fight against the nihilism of contemporary society and to resist a reduction of man, who is a being of desire, who gives meaning and who is above all free, to the level of a mere consumer and a unit of production and of social and economic exchange.

Christian theologians cannot, however, try, in theory, to elaborate an idea of man as a spiritual subject open to God without being committed, in praxis, to setting the whole man free. The Church must therefore fight consciously against all contemporary forms of dehumanization. The discredit into which humanism has fallen should not divert Christians from their struggle for man, a struggle which must be conducted in the presence of the claims of humanism and of man's destiny. In this struggle, Christians will be better equipped than other men if they are convinced that totalitarianism, money, the ruling class or the State are not the only causes of man's alienation. Man is also enslaved to death and to nothingness in all its forms.

II. The Contributions to this Number

In view of what I have said so far, it should cause no surprise that there are few directly theological contributions to this number of *Concilium*. Theologians have, after all, to learn how to work on the frontiers of their discipline and in close co-operation with other disciplines. Before trying too hastily to synthesize, they might do better to accept the disorientation that they may experience in their encounter with the most characteristic expressions of contemporary society.

This number, then, opens with a series of articles written by non-theologians and without purely theological considerations in mind. In the first, J.-M. Domenach points out the complex historical causes and the many ways in which the process of social change is expressed. This is followed by an attempt to understand the "historical" significance of the application of the linguistic model to such humane sciences as ethnology, sociology and psychoanalysis. Despite its technical nature, L. Marin's article on the Saussurian linguistic model is therefore indispensable from the methodological point of view. It may help us to understand

why the "object" of the humane sciences cannot be constructed
by destroying man as the one who gives meaning.

E. Cornélis's article on the image of man in the Indian tradition
will show us how relative our purely Western idea of man is.
He also puts us on our guard against contrasting in too easy a
way Western and Eastern man. A. de Waelhens writes about the
transformation of our traditional image of man brought about by
psychoanalysis and reminds us that we must be cautious when
we speak about anti-humanism in connection with the humane
sciences. Psychoanalytical theory and praxis form a very difficult
apprenticeship to the truth of the human reality.

In his philosophical article, G. Granel shows that he favours a
modern interpretation of metaphysics. His definition of the task
of modern philosophy as a struggle against the subject may cause
some surprise, but it is hardly possible to challenge the radical
nature of his question, which is likely to open our minds to an
understanding of the change that is taking place within Western
society.

Having allowed those specializing in the humane sciences and
in philosophy to speak, we ought to give an historian the opportunity of showing us that the humanistic ideology has not always
been in the service of humanization, but has often concealed or
strengthened a scandalously inhuman situation. Unfortunately,
the author whom we asked to contribute this article was not able
to do so at the last moment.

A. Ganoczy and W. Pannenberg do not, in their theological
contributions, try to make a premature and therefore perhaps
illusory synthesis between the new image of man and the Christian anthropology. On the contrary, they each show how the
current changes that are taking place in our traditional image of
man should stimulate us to concentrate again on the original
character of Christian man as made in the image of perfect man,
Jesus Christ.

Finally, the bulletins in this number on humanism in question
are concerned with the changes in the view that modern man
has of himself (G. Crespy and A. Gibson) or with the part played
by humanism in the dialogue between atheism and Christianity
(J.-Y. Jolif and Y. Labbé).   CLAUDE GEFFRÉ
Translated by David Smith

PART I
ARTICLES

Jean-Marie Domenach

The Attack on Humanism
in Contemporary Culture

LIKE all words ending in "ism", "humanism" is a late coinage whose meaning has remained vague. In literature it denotes the Renaissance movement which took from the Greek and Latin writers an image of man as learned and moral, capable of regenerating a civilization and purging it of its "barbarism". Philosophically, the word denotes those doctrines which stress the dignity of the human person: "Humanism", wrote Sartre at the end of the Second World War, "may be understood to mean a theory which takes man as its end and highest value." There is a difference between these two senses, but perhaps also an important connection.

In fact, the term "humanism" is much later than "humanist", and, as is often the case, the movement towards laudatory or pejorative began with the adjective. And indeed, since the humanist offered himself as a model of man, it was not unfair that the first questioning of the theory should have been directed at its finished, incarnate model. The humanist, a man of wide culture, comprehensive, tolerant, was seen as a "noble soul", full of ineffectual principles, a hypocritical servant of the "bourgeois" system; it was only a short step from there to an attack on his religion, the religion of man. Only lately respected, humanism has now been branded an archaic conviction. The defenders of the classical idea of man no longer dare to acknowledge their creed, and their opponents wave the word around with scorn as a symbol for intellectual senility.

This reversal has taken place in a mere fifteen years. In 1945

Sartre could call a famous lecture "Existentialism is a Human-ism".[1] Emerging from the terror of a war in which the very idea of a human race had almost been destroyed, existentialism, in terms identical to Marxism and Christianity, claimed to be a humanism. The argument between the three was of course fierce, but it took place on common ground; its premise was a definition of man. It is this common ground, the meaning of this definition and its object, man, which have been under attack for fifteen years. A combined attack was launched on humanism (note that its opponents gave it this unity, humanism, not humanisms) under the leadership of Louis Althusser's neo-Marxism, Jean Lacan's neo-Freudianism, the neo-positivism of Claude Lévi-Strauss and Michel Foucault and with the support of the heirs of Heideggerian ontology. These philosophies are clearly different from each other and sometimes incompatible, but from our point of view that is secondary. The important point is that they define themselves by opposition to a traditional set of problems which they denote by the repugnant name of humanism, that they each proclaim in their different ways "the rejection of lived experi-ence, the destruction of man".[2]

Two facts show that this is a cultural phenomenon which goes much deeper than the provocative slogans announcing the death of man. First, the challenge to the personal subject in his identity, conscience and freedom was not in the first place philosophical or scientific, but aesthetic. The *nouveau roman*, the theatre of the absurd and the cinema in the fifties sketched out the motifs and sometimes even the phrases which were to be taken up and de-veloped ten years later by ethnologists, psychoanalysts, biologists and philosophers. The vision of a deserted planet, a doomed race and the disappearance of the individual has been current for more than twenty years in *avant-garde* works of high quality. "I do not exist. The fact is notorious," says one of Samuel Beckett's charac-ters. Beckett's first novels were written immediately after the Second World War. So too the characters of Ionesco or Robbe-Grillet;

[1] A good illustration of the shift of meaning of the word "humanism" is that Simone de Beauvoir in *The Force of Circumstance*, without notic-ing, turned the title of this lecture into a question, "Is existentialism a humanism?". The word was already beginning to become suspect in 1963.
[2] M. Dufrenne, *Pour l'homme* (Paris, 1968), p. 10.

do they exist in anything like the same way as normal men, have they any more existence than Giacometti's bronze spectres? In one sense sculpture and painting were the forerunners, fifty years before, of that elimination of the human figure which Foucault was to describe at the end of *Mots et les choses* (1966), of that agony of entropy of mankind which Lévi-Strauss describes at the end of *L'Homme nu* (1971), of the general mechanization of space which G. Deleuze and F. Guattari made the theme of their *L'Anti-Oedipe* (1972). Think only of Picasso, Max Ernst, Chirico.

The second social fact which includes a philosophical criticism of humanism is the speed with which theories which are subtle and often hardly understood by their adherents have won a large audience among the intelligentsia.[3] Sartre attributed the amazing success of *Mots et les choses*, a particularly difficult book, to the fact that it was "expected", and inferred a deep correspondence between the theses of structuralism and the dominant ideology of the period, technocracy. This form of interpretation needs to be handled with care, even when used against those who abuse it, but nevertheless the way in which the thought of certain writers (Lévi-Strauss, Foucault, Althusser, Barthes) has crystallized into an intellectual fashion is revealing. In spite of these writers' objections to the common label "structuralist" which has been applied to them, it is still true that a large number of French intellectuals have combined these different outlooks into a single ideology, the core of which is an anti-humanism, which is one of their genuine elements and which corresponded to an implicit state of mind which they both revealed and stimulated. When the mood of a period is looking for an ideology it finds philosophical contradictions and objections no barrier, but manufactures a smooth honey from the most dissimilar flowers, showing an indisputable instinct for the spirit of the age, which in this case is firmly anti-humanist.

This generally and instinctively hostile view gives us a point at which we can link the two semantic branches of humanism and see it once more as a totality. The public success of extremely complicated theories which demonstrate the broad scientific and philosophical learning of their authors and, as in the cases of

[3] The intelligentsia is much greater today than in the last century and influences large categories, such as teachers.

Foucault, Lévi-Strauss and Barthes, reach the level of literature, contrasts in appearance with the decline of the "humanities", the classical curriculum which draws on Greek and Latin sources, but it is no more than appearance. In the first place, it is well known that those who most powerfully reject a culture are its most perfect products—this was particularly clear in the eighteenth century. Again, university students find in these refined formulations a confirmation of their own revolt which is at once radical and reassuring. It is radical because it denies the principle of humanism which the authorities try to instil in them, reassuring because they can—or think they can—understand this negation, which in a confused way confirms them in that membership of an intellectual aristocracy which it used to be the function of a classical education to confer. To deny man with machine-guns and concentration camps, or simply with obscene screams (it is sometimes tried), has a repulsive and traumatic effect. To deny man with a scaffolding of science, professorial serenity and cultivated phrases gives an impression of progress rather than regression. Hence the feeling of cheerful superiority. Humanism is ransacked with its own techniques—why bother any more with all the effort to appropriate what can be so deliciously consumed in its own destruction?

Detecting this disturbing ambiguity does not remove the need to measure the extent of the cultural shift which is taking place. Just as in the eighteenth century a break took place with the humanism of the Renaissance, so today we are in the process of breaking with the humanism which reformed in the eighteenth century, though that was an unstable compound, since so many elements of the present anti-humanism first appeared in fact in the nineteenth century, with the beginning of large-scale industry and proletarianization. The boredom which hangs over the classes where Homer, Cicero, Goethe, Racine or Victor Hugo are taught proves that a mode of communication has been broken. The staple values of our tradition are criticized more and more, and the current arguments about marriage, abortion, culture, and so on, show that in spite of two revolutions, the French and the Russian, and a century of secularization (in France at least), those values were basically Christian—even the attack on Christianity has been made in the name of Christian values. It is true

that Greek tragedy has provided models which have not ceased
to be interpreted and reapplied by both the classics and the
romantics and by Marx, Nietzsche and Freud. But if Oedipus
has become a complex, Freud's morality remains fundamentally
bourgeois and almost puritan. It was with Wilhelm Reich that
psychoanalysis joined the counter-culture, and Deleuze attacks it
today as the last sanctuary of the family, the traditional cell of
society. And if Marx rediscovered the figure of Prometheus in
the proletariat, it is none the less true that alienation, the proletariat as universal saviour and, more generally, the vision of
the nations moving towards reconciliation were transcriptions of
Christianity.

This brings us back to an almost forgotten truth. If humanism
appears to us today as more or less allied with Christianity, its
real declaration at its origin was against Christianity. It reversed
its principles and reinterpreted its teaching. Even the word
"humanism" was first used in its modern sense in France by
Proudhon in 1852. Proudhon, like Marx, held that man would
never achieve his full potential unless he freed himself from his
God. For Blanqui socialism was "the gospel in action". Curiously,
humanism, denounced today as an illusion and an excuse, then
proclaimed itself the champion of praxis in opposition to a mysti-
fying theism. In its second wave, in the twentieth century, humanism is also seen by Sartre and Camus as the necessary consequence
of atheism—only the death of God gives man the right to become
a value for man. According to Proudhon, atheism begins when
man feels himself better than his God. In reality, however, what
was taking place was a battle for the sacred, for the supreme
value. It is clear to us today that both sides were fighting on the
same ground for the same stronghold.

We see a strange transposition. Humanism, formed in a half-
pagan, half-Christian context, turned, after the beginning of the
eighteenth century, into an atheist doctrine, but today it is anti-
humanism which presents itself as atheistic, while Christianity,
and especially the Catholic Church since Vatican II, is claiming
to be a humanism.[4] This phenomenon points to an inversion so
far little appreciated in ideological and moral positions. The

[4] Remember Paul VI's introduction of himself to the U.N. General
Assembly as "an expert in humanity".

theoretical debate between Christians and Marxists, for example, recently so lively, now flags, at least in Western Europe, and there are even the beginnings of a sort of common front between Christians and Marxists for the defence of traditional values, culture, work, the nation, the family.

A similar reversal has taken place in the relations between humanism and the socio-economic situation. Whereas, in a period of poverty and under an oppressive regime, humanism appeared and still often appears, as progressive, it appears as reactionary in a period of abundance, in the permissive societies coming into being in the West. This is the source of a confusion which puzzles the fugitives from communist countries. After having suffered for the sake of human rights, they cannot understand why a civilization should seem to deny the principles on which it is based and which give it prestige in the eyes of the persecuted, freedom of thought, tolerance, respect for individual conscience, concern for truth, pity—all the sentiments of "humanity" which have disappeared from French literature since the death of Albert Camus but are the essential of the message of Solzhenitsyn.

We must put our analysis into perspective. The attack on humanism seems to be linked with a certain technical, economic, social and political stage, in general that of the liberal democracies symbolized by the affluent society. In contrast, cultural awakening in underdeveloped countries and opposition among people subjected to dictatorships of right or left appeal to the traditional values of humanism. This protest can sometimes seem worn and conventional, but a fact which should put us on our guard against concluding too hastily to the "death of man" is that the greatest living novelist (or one of the greatest), Solzhenitsyn, has created astounding works on the basis of the simplest principles of humanism. Wherever people struggle against oppression they base their struggle on "humanist" values, on the right of peoples and individuals to live in freedom, even if they have adopted Marxism as a mobilizing ideology.[5] There has never been seen—nor will there ever be—a structuralist re-

[5] It is striking that in the U.S.S.R., Czechoslovakia, Greece, Brazil, etc., it is the intellectuals (in the widest sense) in particular who are resisting and are objects of repression.

sistance. When one has to risk one's life or simply choose sides, the question arises, "in the name of what?", and it cannot be answered by theories which eliminate all reference to values. No science will ever provide a basis for ethics. No system which abolishes man will ever give man reasons for revolt. But so strong is the pull of fashion that this simple objection is never even considered.

Nevertheless, though it may be true that any culture can always be related to its historical determinants and given a place in a wider system of knowledge (and what a temptation to apply this synthesis to theories which claim to make use of it for their own advantage!), we do not wish to use this method to discredit the central claims of anti-humanism. To do so would be to adopt a determinism or a dialectical tension to which we do not subscribe, and our undertaking would be in bad faith.

I believe that, while taking account of the ambiguities of this anti-humanism and of the enormous ideological element it contains, we must try to submit ourselves to its criticism, to its discipline (in both the intellectual sense of a study and the traditional Catholic sense of a whip). We may regard the world of culture as sealed off or capable of being sealed, in which case we are driven into the circle of a closed interpretation, which is characteristic of the various forms of structuralism, or we may believe that, while they form a system within their own period, cultures bring a contribution which must be brought into dialogue with others in a spirit of intellectual ecumenism. In the second case, we have no right to reject our intellectual environment, to run away from our own culture. That, probably, is where the decisive choice between humanism and its opposite lies. By choosing dialogue, that is to say, a humanism in advance of us, I choose the relativity of my own culture and try to accept its challenge. French culture today is the one which takes the attack on humanism furthest. It is not false to connect this with the reduction of France's power and influence,[6] but it is insufficient— history is full of countries in decline which have dominated the world with their genius. If France provides the shock troops of anti-humanism, this is probably because the French have a pro-

[6] Cf. F. Furet, "Les intellectuels français et le structuralisme", *Preuves* (Feb. 1967).

pensity for sharpening intellectual trends and making them more abstract, and also because France's rapid development makes it more receptive—the transition from the rural to the industrial stage in a country with an old culture is traumatic. These, in my opinion, are the reasons why we should take anti-humanism seriously in the provocative form it assumes in France.

"Before having the idea of the death of man, our age lived it."[7] It is true that the last world war and the concentration camps, the genocide and ethnocide it brought with it and famine, world poverty and the prospect of an atomic war form a context which we should keep in mind when we talk about humanism. One could say roughly that the plastic arts had an intuition, as early as the beginning of the century, of what mankind would have to live through, and only later did verbal culture begin to picture the death of man, particularly in the novels, plays and films of the fifties and lastly in the theories of the death of man which were developed in the sixties. It is of course impossible to divide these stages up into separate periods, because they interact with each other, just as the discovery of pollution has taken up and amplified the fear of suicide of the human race provoked by the explosion at Hiroshima.

The sixties was the decade in which France entered the consumer society and began to become urbanized at an increasing rate. This phenomenon is illustrated in novels and plays. The man we see there feels himself becoming a thing among other things; he is falling, falling apart.[8] Submerged by affluence, slotted into a mechanized universe, he begins to be afraid and feel unnecessary. As he is more and more surrounded by instruments which measure and monitor him, he finds himself "standardized". There is a paradox here. The image of dehumanization in art and literature both conceals and helps to reveal the fear of no longer being oneself, especially in a country like France, where the old hierarchies were till recently vigorous. It is as though the search for identity which grew up with the industrial era, after wandering in search of collective entities, such as the nation, the class and the race, was trying unconsciously to find comfort in a

---

[7] Dufrenne, op. cit., p. 229.
[8] It is interesting to apply here Heidegger's ontological analysis of decline, his Verfall.

bitter consolation: "Man no longer exists; you have been chasing a reflection, a dream."

If we regard the post-war existentialist period as a parenthesis, an offshoot of the old humanism which soon withered, we find that the destruction of man begun by totalitarianism has been continued in a new way by the industrial societies, and the new culture stands in this line. In Beckett, whose work goes back to before the war, and Ionesco there is no discontinuity at all between the disfigurement of man by Nazism and by post-war mechanized society. It is no longer an individual family or hero who is caught in the trap and crushed, as in Greek tragedy, but humanity in its essence.

In 1958 Alain Robbe-Grillet published the famous pamphlet in which he attacked the existentialists for surreptitiously reintroducing the human into nature under cover of the absurd, which was a new manifestation of the tragic, that is to say of the old humanism.[9] Robbe-Grillet claimed that the novel ought to describe man as an object, at the most as an insect among insects. This was an aesthetic rather than a philosophical position which was to be maintained after a fashion by the authors associated with the *nouveau roman*. Considerable skill, of which Robbe-Grillet was to be for a time the master, succeeded in removing from the character all his individual characteristics, down to his name and the idea of his identity.[10] Both author and character disappear, leaving a closed system which abolishes history and time. This ambivalent achievement lasted no more than a decade, but was a true prototype of many of the features of the emerging structuralism. There is a further point here which illuminates the connection between the two senses of the word "humanism". It was the destruction of the "hero" which was a prelude to the execution of man carried out by the neo-positivism which the social sciences had created. There was no longer any need for a character with nobility or any sort of supremacy (the ambiguity of the word "hero" is revealing, as in military hero and literary hero), because there was no need for a character at all: just

---

[9] Alain Robbe-Grillet, "Nature, humanisme et tragedie", *Nouvelle Revue française* (October 1958).
[10] See in particular *La Jalousie* and *Les Gammes*.

"someone", not a man. Elimination of the name led to total elimination, negation of value to negation of existence.

This fall to the "degree zero" of humanity is admirably illustrated by Samuel Beckett's works and by Ionesco's early plays.[11] Their characters are the rejects of humanity, or at least vulgar, vapid creatures. They are also "unnamables",[12] or nameless, beings whose only autonomy is their voice. How, they ask, can one retain identity in a world constantly changing? How can one act, how can one do or be anything in a society in which motivation is dissolved by meaninglessness? How can one communicate when one is abandoned to the competition of production and consumption? How can one love? Beckett's masterpiece, *Happy Days*,[13] has given us the image of this dereliction, the woman bogged down in the desert and clutching at fragments of memories. The negation of man is probably inseparable from the proliferation of the species. The more the race grows and crowds in on itself, the greater becomes the isolation, the fear of the other and the wish to destroy him. Three and a half thousand million human beings. "This land might be inhabited," as one of Beckett's characters says.

These creatures who have lost everything, youth and beauty, past and future, still at least have language. "Words, there's nothing else" (Beckett). But these words which keep Winnie alive in *Happy Days* are "other people's words". The *nouveau roman*, the theatre of the absurd and Beckett in particular are predecessors of Foucault and Lacan with this twofold revelation. Firstly, the classical hero is dead, both as a literary character or a philosophical subject, the one who both expressed values and himself stood out as supreme value. Secondly, man no longer speaks—he is spoken. "Where once the 'I' occupied the place of honour in the system of artistic portrayals, language now utters his truth before him."[14] It was of course in language that Beckett and

---

[11] There is no room here for a proper distinction between these two authors. Ionesco, in fact, has never ceased to be a humanist, and this is shown by his position in current controversies.

[12] One of Beckett's books is called *The Unnamable* (New York, 1958: original edition, *L'Innomable*, Paris, 1953).

[13] London and New York, 1961.

[14] M. de Certeau, "Les sciences humaines et la mort de l'homme", *Etudes* (March 1967).

Ionesco placed man's agony, his last battle. Now Beckett has been reduced to silence, while structural analysis has taken language to pieces and put it together again as a self-sufficient circuit of which man is the receiver and amplifier.

Literature had already tried to escape from rational discourse. The surrealists had drawn on the unconscious. Antoine Artaud had directed the theatre towards cruelty. Gradually, we saw spectacles of increasing savagery. Screams, violence and gestures have replaced speech. The naked man has appeared on our stages and screens, a preview of the ethnological savage whom Lévi-Strauss was to make an essential element of the negation of humanism. Now we have reached the final stage. If man is deprived of the human faculty *par excellence*, the power to give meaning, does there not exist speech from outside, like Foucault's "thought from outside"? Deleuze and Guattari rely on schizophrenic raving to subvert the natural and social orders; this is the "anti-world", of which one of Ionesco's characters said, "there is no proof that it exists, but by thinking about it we find it in our own thought". From this point the targets within humanism are no longer only values and a culture, but the claim to coherence of discourse, no longer just the sovereignty of the individual subject but reason itself. Is this the beginning of a fruitful recovery of the "beyond", of all that has been excluded and cheapened by bourgeois culture, in the manner of Hölderlin and Rimbaud? This "death of the cultural"[15] has no future except in culture itself unless it is to lead into "the violence of pure reciprocity", the jungle, and the breaking of the human species into irreconcilable fragments. As Nietzsche said, only art offers an escape when thought has reached the end of nihilism. It is the irrefutable evidence that man exists, that in spite of everything man continues even when freedom and meaning are negated.

In this way culture helps us to measure the importance of the attack on humanism from two extremes, from the one towards which humanism itself tends, rationalization and automation, and from the one which it thought it had driven back by civilization and destruction, savagery. The attack is ambiguous, as we have seen, because it appeals to contradictory realities: structural

[15] René Girard, "Système du délire", *Critique* (Nov. 1972).

ethnology was produced by a programme based on primitives. No doubt in fact this contradiction is only apparent. If the highest levels of programmed analysis and scientific argument join forces with the barbarism of the counter-culture to proclaim the death of humanism, this shows that humanism itself had already reached an even more serious contradiction, that between its proclaimed values and the ravages of its industrial and military technology. Stripped of his clothes, his normal language, his claims to absoluteness, and also of his ignorance, man staggers under the order, "Now tell us who you are." He may for a moment have thought he was a god, but to answer the question he will have to go on asking for a long time yet. Even the Son of God, asked a similar question, had no clear answer.

Translated by Francis McDonagh

Louis Marin

The Disappearance of Man in the Humane Sciences—A Linguistic Model and Signifying Subject

MICHEL FOUCAULT, echoing Nietzsche's prophecy of the death of God in a phrase that made quite an impression in its time, announced the death of man.[1] Man's mortality is of course as well known to the man in the street as to the philosopher, so a thinker of Foucault's stature must have been doing rather more than lend his name to a re-affirmation of an obvious truth: he was in fact stating a truth somewhat less easy to grasp—one concerning the humane sciences, and making an attempt to give them what one can only call a metaphysical basis.

Founding a science involves producing the title deeds of its genuine claim to truth, and showing the conditions under which it is possible to practise it; if the death of man is to be one of the conditions for practising the humane sciences, then there is undoubtedly a paradox, and one that leaves plenty of room for examination of the conditions that have made its formulation possible. The affirmation of the death of man is then perhaps a literary expression of the truth of the scientific process itself. Just as geometric space in a way involves "the death" of existential space, the physical object, so the "space" in which the varieties of feeling and intuition operate—a certain global and immediate sense of humanity, the irresistible witness of conscience in regard to states of mind and their expression, experience lived as a meaningful whole by an individual or a group—must give way to the results of investigations that can only function by breaking

---

[1] M. Foucault, *Les mots et les choses* (Paris, 1967).

with this intuition, witness and experience. So, man dies in the very sciences that take him as their object because their object as such can only be built up *against* global intuitions, spontaneous expressions and immediate impressions.

The problem then becomes one of finding out what the object of these sciences actually is, what processes form it, what sort of relationship it sustains with observable facts, with the elements of experience, with individual and collective images whose sum and transformation it represents. Is "man" an idea that governs the human sciences, in the Kantian sense of the term, an idea that would set the boundaries to the processes of objectivization, a transcendental illusion to be dissipated by scientific investigation itself (without ceasing to recognize its inescapable force)? Or is he rather a necessary constituent, characteristic of a particular historical moment, of a contextual "understanding" of the humane sciences? If this question connects with that of the basis of a science mentioned earlier, it remains true that it can only be asked if we start from a critical examination of the scientific process itself. The question is at once the means and the end of the investigation.

What is the process by which the experience man lives is structured? How can we construct a model that will represent the facts? What are the rules that govern the construction of such a model? What sorts of relationships exist between the different models that we can build to represent the object? These questions are in turn governed, separately and together, by an historical fact of undoubted transcendental significance. Where humane sciences are concerned, the processes of constructing models to structure experience are dominated by the model of one particular human science—linguistics, the paradigmatic position of which is in some way inherent in reflection on language as a science.

In other words, the models that linguistics has been constructing for almost a hundred years will also serve as models in another sense—they will provide the other humane sciences with hypotheses, concepts, means of operating. These will be relevant to sciences such as ethnology, sociology, psychoanalysis, even biology. If one asks how one particular science can provide models for the structuring of other sciences, is this not implied by the characteristics of the concepts of sign, language, speech, not to mention the theoretical production of the means of communication and exchange? This is how I would justify setting the limits of this examination of the dissolution of man in the humane sciences: an investigation into the nature and position of the signifying subject in the formation of the structural model of language as formulated by Ferdinand de Saussure.

His linguistics, in a truly Copernican revolution, is made up of a double break with tradition, in both methodology and aim. In methodology, by claiming that linguistics can be established as a science only by rigorously separating the synchronic from the diachronic, the structural from the historical; in aim: by defining this as to distinguish, from within the anomalous mass of the facts of language—individual and collective, physical, psychological and sociological—one homogeneous, observable object which should be singled out as first constituent of a systematic whole. But the movement by which linguistics defined its methodological procedures was the same as that by which it structured its aim: "The reality of the object could not be separated from the correct method of defining it".[2] Or, as defined at the beginning of the *Course of General Linguistics*: "the task of linguistics must be: (a) to describe the structure and history of all the languages it can reach; (b) to find out the forces that are permanently in operation and permanent in all languages; and (c) to set its limits and define itself".[3]

The first two tasks are resolutely subordinated to the third, and this is the same as the basic question posed by Saussure: "What is the integral and at the same time particular aim of linguistics?"[4] The historical research that aims at "tracing the history of each family of languages and reconstructing as far as possible the mother tongues of each group" is integrated as part of the theory underlying the system of "general laws to which all the particular phenomena of history can be related", and this theory is based on the articulation of adequate procedures and criteria for a description of the linguistic object, procedures and criteria that belong to linguistics alone and do not stem from other

[2] E. Benvéniste, *Problèmes et linguistique générale* (Paris, 1966), p. 166.
[3] F. de Saussure, *Cours de linguistique générale* (Paris, 3rd edn., 1965), p. 20.
[4] *Ibid.*, p. 23.

sciences. It is through them that linguistics is delineated and defines itself; this operation is the same as that of posing the structure of its aim. While "other sciences operate with aims defined in advance and which can then be considered from different points of view", it is the inseparable duality of method and aim that makes linguistics a science and makes its aim a formal structure or at least one capable of being formalized. "Rather than the aim preceding the point of view, it is the point of view that creates the aim."[5]

So Saussure's Copernican revolution consists basically in stating that language is neither a substance, nor an organism in the course of evolution, nor a free creation of man's, but a constituent *relationship* between a *method* of knowing and an *object* to be known. The scientific aim is a specific structuring operated by a body of methodological procedures and criteria, and, reciprocally, this body is no more than the complex operative projection of this aim. Our only knowledge of language is of the models of it we make and we only know these to the extent that we make them through a rigorous process of structuring: "language is a whole in itself as well as a principle of classification".[6] Language is defined both *a parte rei*, as a systematic whole, and *a parte intellectus*, as a principle of knowledge—it is only a systematic whole because it is a principle of knowledge and *vice versa*. It is both a model and an operative complex of models. In other words, it is a formal structure.

The opposition between what signifies and what is signified, between language and the word, stems from this all-embracing theoretical conception that relationships exist before things themselves, that things are "effects" or products of the dual relationship in which they generate themselves in their own existence both reciprocally and differentially.

Hence the two criticisms to which Saussure's theories are open —the first of the process by which linguistics is said to be its own basis and definition and the second of the structures of opposition. In fact, if language does not contain any substantial reality, but consists entirely of differences because there are no positive terms for differences to establish themselves between, then it is

[5] *Ibid.*, p. 23.   [6] *Ibid.*, p. 25.

right that the basic unities of the system *define themselves*: the marks, characteristics and descriptive propositions by which a sign can be said to be such become, in themselves, the sign itself. The sign is nothing more than the descriptive operation that enables it to be known. And linguistics, in defining the unities of language, does delineate and define itself; its aim is defined as it builds itself up. "The characteristics of the whole are confused with the whole itself. In language, as in any semeiological system —and we shall see the importance of this specification—what distinguishes a sign is all that it is. Difference gives it its character, as it gives it its value and its unity."[7] As Ogden and Richards have pointed out, in their attack on Saussure in the name of logical empiricism, the process of interpreting the sign is included in the sign itself. They see this as a vicious circle and, in the final analysis, sheer imagination,[8] but it is possible to take it as a constitutive operation of immense significance for the humane sciences, in that it rediscovers the basic circular movement in which Hegel resumes the philosophical system. In this sense, Saussure's linguistics can claim to act as a basic model for the humane sciences, since it is the fundamental science in the sense that it is but its own object acceding to a known consciousness of itself. So the concept of system is basic to Saussure's thought, every object of linguistics finding its reality only in the play of differences that constitute the relationships underlying the whole system.

The second criticism bears on the structures of opposition between what signifies and what is signified, finding in them the reified poles characteristic of ideological representations: Saussure's linguistic model re-creates the old oppositions between body and soul, thought and matter. It is certainly true that a popularized "Saussure-ism" has become inflexible along these lines. The difficult concept of the generative difference of terms between which the difference exists has been replaced by a substantialist mode of thought in which each of the terms has independence as a thing, and the relationship between them is external to them. It is true that Saussure explained in the *Course* that the word is an individual act of will and intelligence. In defining language,

[7] *Ibid.*, p. 168.
[8] C. K. Ogden and I. A. Richards, *The Meaning of Meaning* (London, 1960), p. 5, n. 2.

in opposition to this, as a social and collective object, as a contractual code or tie, as a whole in fact, the word can easily come to be seen as a part of this whole, just as an individual is part of the social structure.

The only way out of these difficulties, of understanding the dual relationship characterizing language on all levels, would seem to be to see it as a relationship that is both systematic and dialectic—systematic because it is dialectic, and dialectic because it is systematic.[9] The exceptional strength of Saussure's approach seems to me that it adds the contradictory relationship that constitutes language to self-knowledge and finds the basis of the science of linguistics in this contradiction. If language is a pure system, this means that it is made up of differences and nothing else. The sum of these differences produces the actuality of the system of values that lies at the origin of language. This actuality is both complex and paradoxical because it is made up of opposites that themselves stem from the differences, where one will never "find anything simple, but always and everywhere this same complex equilibrium of reciprocally self-conditioning terms".[10] The statement that language is a total system of differences, in which meaning is produced through opposites, is an affirmation of its dialectical character and, by the same token, of the dialectical nature of scientific knowledge of it. So Saussure's formal and systematic linguistics is a dialectical linguistics through making itself such in the process of establishing an object that is dialectical in itself.

This can be seen through an examination of the relationship between language and word in the *Course*. "To find the sphere corresponding to each tongue in the whole complex of language, one has to consider the individual act that allows one to establish the circuit of the word. This act requires at least two individuals. This is the minimum requirement for completion of the circuit."[11]

---

[9] See on this point, Mikuš, "La linguistique de Sapir", in *Cahiers F. de Saussure* (Geneva, No. 11, 1953); N. Slusereva, "Quelques considérations des linguistes soviétiques à propos des idées de F. de Saussure", in *ibid.*, No. 20, 1963; F. Jameson, *The Prison House of Language: a Critical Account of Structuralism and Russian Formalism* (Princeton, 1972), pp. 3–39.

[10] F. de Saussure, *op. cit.*

[11] *Ibid.*

So we are left with this question, where does a language exist and how objective is its existence? Note that in order to answer this question, Saussure turns to analysis of the concrete structure of the word as relationship between two speakers. In place of the substantialist concept of a language as a reservoir of collective signs and rules in the individual mind, and of words as the individual's actual expression of some of the elements in this reservoir, he gives us a phenomenological and dialectical concept of the word circuit in which the word is at once the fact of the transmitter of the language, the fact of the receiver of the message, and its understanding and interpretation.

Language is then in the word, as the word is in language: "there can be no words except through the elaboration of the product called language, which provides the individual with the elements out of which to make up his words".[12] The relationship between word and language is a dialectical one, and this is why Saussure tackles it first as a relationship in dialogue, in the process of exchange and communication. Language is the power of understanding the word; the word is the power of producing language. Both appear concretely at the two poles of the circuit, without either depending on any particular ontological and substantial speaking subject, since in the process of exchange, both the power of understanding words and the power of producing language belong in their turn fully and of right to the speakers engaged in the exchange. In order to explain this more fully, to prove this relationship between word and language scientifically, Saussure is of course forced to move beyond phenomenological description of the process of exchange. But the series of definitions of language he gives in the *Course* confirms the dialectical nature of the theoretical relationship since the object known through this relationship is itself dialectical by nature. The model built up by linguistics is constructed in the form of dialogue, just as the dialogue was itself described in terms of a model.

What the Copernican circle of Saussure's linguistics teaches us is that the dialectic does not necessarily and immediately mean history first and (personal) subject second, nor that it means them in another way. Dialectic means synchronic system and formal

[12] R. Godel, *Sources manuscites du Cours de linguistique générale* (Geneva, 1957), p. 155.

structure, synchronic system to the extent that the object that emerges from the dialectical process of scientific definition is made up of relationships, which, in their particular order, generate the terms that relate them. By defining language as a value, Saussure is in fact defining it as perception of an identity, but this perception of identity (which is a perception of meaning) is the same thing as the perception of difference. When I *identify* a fragment of language through its meaning, this means precisely that I am *differentiating* it from all the rest of the language. And the definition of the dialectical process in that identity is difference, which is also what happens in fact in the system.

Furthermore, if each element of language as a constitutive unity cannot be distinguished from the others by what it represents or designates, then meaning cannot be constituted by the extrinsic relationship between sign and reality, by the label that a word, for example, puts on an object. It must be produced by the internal constituent relationship this word enjoys with all the other words in the vocabulary of this language. This is how we arrive at a definition of the formal structure of language, as the totality formed by particular, basically binary, relationships— formal to the extent that these relationships are not external to the elements they link together, but constituent parts of these elements.

We can now go back to the original break made by Saussure with preceding linguistics and examine the question of history and the subject. Saussure's Copernican revolution was initially— as we have seen—the rigorous separation of the synchronic from the diachronic, the structural from the historical. This dates from the famous "Memoir on the primitive vowel system of the Indo-European languages", which still derives to a certain extent from historical linguistics. But the same dialectical process is evident in it—if linguistics must be synchronic in order to be scientific, it cannot become so except through a relationship with the diachronic. "The synchronic should be treated on its own, but without making the continual opposition between it and the diachronic, one gets nowhere. The ancient grammarians had a fine time producing static linguistics, but what did they actually achieve?"[13] What scientific approach, then, will correspond to

[13] *Ibid.*, p. 186.

the theoretical dialectical attitude that we have seen traced at each level of linguistic knowledge and aim? It will consist in taking meaning as its guideline. "Meaning is the basic condition that any unity and any level must fulfil in order to achieve the linguistic status . . . meaning is an indispensable condition of linguistic analysis. One only has to see how meaning comes into our investigations, and the level of analysis it derives from".[14] Meaning, "the basic synchronic fact", is defined as "the act of communication", the circuit made by words, "the phrase by which a listener is enabled to take in a significance. . . . To recognize a linguistic fact in a series of meanings, one must have a listener who understands their significance."[15]

These linguistic propositions are basic to an understanding of the double problem of history and the subject. How does one solve scientifically the problem of a "passage from one state to another in a continuous process"? History, surely, makes us "become part, outside ourselves, of the very being of change".[16] Or rather, this image of history can be seen as the projection of evidence of the conscient subject in the very act of grasping his being, which he experiences at once as the same and as other and so in this too as the very being of change. And this is the very problem posed so clearly by the dialectic of the diachronic and the synchronic. There is no denying the diachronic fact that sounds and meaning change and change continuously. "There are no permanent features, there are only studies of language in a perpetual state of transition between yesterday and tomorrow."[17] But in the dialectic of exchange, there is only one meaning at any given moment in the history of a language: "words are without memory".[18]

From this follows—through one of the paradoxes Saussure seemed to delight in and which are really no more than the dialectical paradoxes of science and language—that the synchronic is "ontologically" based on the actual experience of com-

[14] E. Benvéniste, op. cit., p. 122.
[15] E. Buyssens, "La linguistique synchronique de F. de Saussure", in Cahiers, No. 18, 1961, pp. 29–30.
[16] C. Lévi-Strauss, The Savage Mind (London, 1968).
[17] R. Godel, op. cit., p. 39.
[18] F. Jameson, op. cit., p. 6.

municating signs, and that the diachronic can only be known through structuring and comparing states of a language, that is, of moments of communication. Continuous change is not and cannot become the object of knowledge except by introducing the synchronic discontinuity which Saussure finds essentially in the dialectical unity of communication. Hence the simultaneous concept of a synchronic-diachronic history and of a subject who is the place where an exchange takes place, in which a totality that he does not bring about, but which is brought about in him, comes to light and becomes an object of understanding.

So, while language is in the word of the historical subject, it is also separated from it as a synchronic system. As the instrument of a dialectical exercise of language and the object of a theoretical dialectic of the science of language, it realizes the human subject's capacity for producing meaning, but only outside its exercise by the individual speaker. Language is not linguistic theory incarnate in the memory, understanding and will of the individual, but linguistic theory alone can reveal language as that which both allows and rigorously defines the individual's power of free expression. This in turn demonstrates linguistic theory in the communication situation—while remaining totally ignorant of it. "A non-reflective totality, language is a human reason that has its reasons and that man knows not of."[19] It is that other totality in which man finds his apodictic experience of the same.

As I said at the beginning of this article, the historical fact of linguistics being constituted as a science undoubtedly has a transcendental significance and, because of this, the linguistic structuring of the language object serves and ought to serve as a model for the other humane sciences. Saussure himself clearly puts forward this basic proposition, but still with the same dialectical ambiguity that marks all the concepts and operations of linguistics, which is only a branch of a wider science: semeiology, which "is to teach us what signs consist of, what rules govern them. Once discovered, these rules will be applicable to linguistics, which will then be linked to a well-defined branch of human activity."[20]

If the linguistic problem is therefore a semeiological problem,

[19] C. Lévi-Strauss, *op. cit.*   [20] F. de Saussure, *op. cit.*, p. 33.

perhaps language should be studied not only through what it has in common with all other semeiological systems if we are to discover its true nature, but as part of the overall picture of human activities, seen as systems of signs and so approaching their scientific understanding from a semeiological standpoint. If the basic characteristic of human activities and events is that they signify—perhaps, more generally, the basic characteristic of all living beings—then semeiology is the basic science, since it comes into being through constructing models of events and activities as sign systems. Far from language being abolished in society, society is beginning to see itself as a language. . . . These new investigations lead one to think that the basic nature of language—being made up of signs—could also apply to the whole of the social phenomena that make up a culture."[21]

But the movement that would place linguistics in the context of the wider science of semeiology also dialectically reverses the position. The main object of semeiology would be the totality of systems based on the arbitrary nature of the sign. "In fact," Saussure continues, "any means of expression received in a society depends on principle on a collective habit, or on convention, which comes to the same thing. . . ."[22] Language, the object of linguistics, is the semeiological system *par excellence*, being at once "the most complex and most widespread system of expression there is, and also the most characteristic of all". It is the semeiotic system that serves as general interpreter of all other semeiotic systems. By the same token, linguistics, the science that studies language, is, although language is one particular system, at once the model of all semeiology and its basis, through the irreversible semeiotic relationship of interpretation linking it to all other systems—not a logical or ontological relationship of predating, but a dialectical one. To take one example: society contains language as a particular system as a "relationship of insertion" in which the extrinsic dependences of each are objectivized; on the other hand, however, language contains society to the extent that it is the necessary and overall interpreter of all the other systems that make up society and to the extent that these are social and cultural systems only through reproducing,

[21] E. Benvéniste, *op. cit.*, pp. 43–4.
[22] F. de Saussure, *op. cit.*, pp. 100–101.

at a certain level of completeness or complexity, the features and behaviour pattern of the normative structure of the "great semeiotic matrix"—language.

Finally, we must ask what characteristics semeiotic systems other than language display. The answer will be found in the basically dualistic structure of the dialectical nature of structural linguistics and of linguistic structure—that what characterizes a fact, an element, or anything charged with meaning, is that its identity is essentially made up of a relationship to something else. This basic articulation is repeated on all levels and at every degree of complexity—nothing has meaning in itself and by itself. Meaning is a relationship: its "ontology" is a system of references in which it is produced through what it is not. This is the initial contradiction or lack whose reabsorption forms language, symbolic systems and the structure of the process of exchange in general.

This leads us to make two conclusions. The first is that the assimilation of the symbolic systems that characterize human activities in relation to language does not mean identification. Claude Lévi-Strauss, one of the first to examine this question, has put it very clearly: "The system of relationship is a language, but it is not a universal language. . . . Faced with a particular culture, there is always one first question to be asked—is the system systematic?"[23] This question, he goes on, is only absurd when applied to language, since language has to be systematic or it is meaningless. But with other symbolic systems—social organization or art, for example—the question "must be posed the more rigorously the more partial, fragmentary or subjective their signifying value is. . . ." If, on the model of language, symbolic systems can be considered as a complex of operations designed to provide a certain type of communication between individuals and groups, then, whether the messages are formed by wives (relationship), words (language) or goods and services (economy) and provided that the differences are strictly expressed, it is possible to envisage "reaching a level on which it will be possible to move from one system to another, to elaborate, that is, a sort of universal code capable of expressing the properties common to the specific struc-

[23] C. Lévi-Strauss, *Structural Anthropology* (London, 1968).

tures belonging to each aspect".[24] This universal code would come very close to realizing Saussure's assertion of a general semeiology.

The second conclusion is concerned with the object of this study, the question of man as signifying subject and intentionality. This is the question posed by analysing Saussure's linguistics as a dialectical system, by examining the basis of the humane sciences as the circular process going from the interpreting system to the systems interpreted, or the question of meaning as "transposition from one level of language to another, from one language into a different language . . . as a possibility of 'transcoding' ".[25] In this process, the subject must be seen in the light of the model of language and of linguistics, as a dialectical subject —dialectic of science and word—as a dialogal structure of exchange, of transposition and transformation of the symbolic systems among themselves, of the different levels of the symbolic order. When Saussure aims to define the object of linguistics and so delineate and define linguistics itself, he describes the circuit of words between two people, the way an exchange works between the emission of a message and the potentiality of its being understood. This is the signifying subject found in the linguistic model underlying the humane sciences. Man appears not as the subject who provides meaning, but as the place where meaning is produced and manifested, where an exchange takes place, where there is selection and regulated combination of symbolic systems, a field of operations in which these systems are limited and constrain each other in a specific way—a place, a field in which he produces himself in the illusion of his self-creating substance, that we would see as the effect of a dialectic of which he is the privileged operator.

Translated by Paul Burns

[24] *Ibid.*
[25] A. Greimas, *Du sens* (Paris, 1970), p. 13.

Etienne Cornélis

Man in the Indian Classics

IT HAS never occurred to Eastern thinkers to define man as a rational animal. In fact, definitions in general have seldom occurred to the Eastern mind, least of all a definition of man. Not that man was not central in one sense. One could even say that he was generally placed on the same level of creation as that on which, say, Aquinas placed him, at the meeting-point of the angelic spheres and the animal kingdoms. The comparison is valuable, but also misleading in one respect. The genies or gods of the East who occupied the same position as the angels in the West are neither pure spirits nor established for ever in their "higher" position. Nor are animals considered in any sense as deprived of rationality by nature, but only by their equally temporary position, on the scale of possible forms of life.

But in both East and West the situation of man is central in an "ultimate" sense, that is, as regards salvation. It is in this respect, and only in this respect, that it is possible to speak of an Eastern humanism. In this respect also, it is both possible and necessary to attempt the difficult task of a mutual translation of the soteriological ideas of East and West, although the difficulty of the task cannot be underestimated. This article should be read as a warning against any relaxation of rigour in such a confrontation, either by an insufficiently self-critical attitude towards the proofs drawn from one's own culture or by optimism about the discovery of easy methods of liberation in the other.

Such a short article would be in danger of saying nothing at all if it tried to take in the whole of the East at once. It would be condemned to stale clichés or the cheap profundity of "total" views. Who could ever claim to reduce to a single denominator the traditional man of the Veda and the new man of Kabir Toukaram, the ideal men of Confucius and Lao-Tzu, the future man as seen by Sri Aurobindo or Mao?

We shall restrict ourselves to Indian anthropologies, but even then the range is enormous, at least as wide as that of Western ways of looking at man. What are we to do? There is little difficulty, as comparativists of all sorts have shown, in setting out as a diptych the most antithetical features of man as seen by East and West while silently taking its principle of organization from the symbolic and conceptual language of the West alone. The living tissue from which these characters from the other conceptual world draw their meaning in this treatment suffer distortions and lacerations which make it unrecognizable for the oriental whose "humanity" is thus falsely said to be placed. In fact, experience, thought and language connect with each other in a unique way in each culture. Only the way in which the subject lives his relation to the world and other living beings is the Ariadne's thread which can lead us to the heart of his unique being in the world.

At the very outset, there are surprises in store for the Westerner, as, for example, when he realizes that sensory perception is generally understood in Indian thought as resulting from action of the subtle internal principle (*antahkarana*) of the sense in going out to meet the object. This illuminates and gives unexpected content to the commonplace that for the East man and the cosmos are homologues and correspond term for term, with man as a microcosm and the cosmos as a larger version of man. This fact also throws light on the statement in the Upanishads that at the disintegration of the living creature each organ, or, better, each sensible "power" goes back to its natural place within the cosmic organism, of the extension of which it was never really more than an accidental limitation. In this connection it is interesting to consider one of the Upanishad's uses of the Sanskrit word *devata* (divinity). It can refer to a vital function, as in this passage: "breathing in and breathing out did not leave them, though all the other *devata* left them. But thanks to these two the creatures did not perish" (*Satapatha Brah.* 2, 5, 2, 2).

I suggest that this linguistic usage has at least three implications: (a) that the vital functions of the individual as microcosm are regarded as participations in the great "regions" into which the cosmic economy is divided; (b) that the gods too, through their correspondence with the functions of the living creature, do not exercise their power independently of each other, but in dependence on and in the service of the whole; (c) that the individual's ideal in life is to imitate, in the exercise of his faculties, the harmonious co-operation of the cosmic powers. We might almost say that the individual's powers or faculties are only lent to him. At the moment of death they go back to the corresponding elementary powers in the great being which is the cosmos.

The views which prevailed in the time of the *brahmanas* (c. 800 B.C.) naturally underwent considerable modification in the course of time, but they have never ceased to influence the most varied theories of knowledge developed by Indian thinkers.

No less than Greece, ancient India had a moment of intoxication in the enthusiasm of the discovery of the sovereign power of the intellect over the other faculties. India, however, did not let itself be taken over to the same extent by the sort of dogmatism which made Western thought the prisoner of those related enemies, dualistic spiritualism and materialistic monism. In India, sensible knowledge has never on the whole been denied a spiritual quality, and the intellectual faculty has never been regarded as different from and opposed to matter. As a result, epistemologies and anthropologies in India did not develop within the framework of the matter-spirit dichotomy. This distinctive feature of Indian thought is inseparable from its refusal to separate thought from experience.

It is true that there are Indian forms of *gnosis*, doctrines of salvation through knowledge, but they have never taken a purely or even mainly theoretical character. They do not work out a theory except in dependence on and in the service of a practice of contemplation, that is to say of the concentrated experience of the real as a whole (body and spirit, multiplicity and unity, time and eternity). This has been expressed from the beginning of Indian anthroposophical speculation by the theory of interlocking powers. The subtle powers which act through the sense organs are "incorporated" by the power (*manas*) which thinks the forms, and the *manas* itself is dominated by the power of discernment and judgment (*buddih*). At the moment of death each of these powers is hierarchically taken back and reabsorbed by the power which dominates it until finally the consciousness (*buddih*) is itself merged, but without being lost, in the *ātman* which illuminates each conscious act from within but is itself outside any identifiable consciousness. Note the phrase "from within", as the most intimate of witnesses; it is a warning not to let ourselves be too much influenced by the necessary but still deceptive metaphor of the incorporator and the incorporated. The *ātman*, the super-power which dominates and incorporates all the others, acts within each of them to give it its own power.

Even in the absence of the other powers, when they have been scattered by death, life can continue thanks to the *ātman*. In the absence of the *ātman*, however, life vanishes. The aim of ascetic exercises is to bring about during the *yogi*'s lifetime what happens naturally to everyone at the moment of death, the withdrawal of the lower powers into the higher, like the sections of a telescope. Such exercises do not aim at and do not produce an abolition of corporeal or sensible elements, but their sublimation through liberation from the slavery to space and time which normally restricts their operations. Opinions differ from school to school about the stages of the process and means of achieving it, but all are agreed on one point, that the achievement of absolute unity (*kaivalya*, *mokṣa*) does not separate "spirit" from "matter", but gathers all the psychic powers into a single principle which is at once that of intellectual functions and corporeal forms. In the process the powers cease to be determined by partial objects, but do not cease to operate.

Pleasure and pain are little more than surface impressions, incapable of really affecting a person who is in a state of perfect recollection. The lotus position adopted by the *yogi* who is trying to reach *samādhi* is painful. It brings on cramps and other discomforts, but the *yogi* takes no notice because the consciousness of pain will in due course give way to a succession of more and more pleasant levels of consciousness which are finally submerged in a deep consciousness in comparison to which all other levels of consciousness are merely degrees of distance or approximation. Once he has reached this consciousness he recognizes it at once, and also recognizes at once that it was always there.

Rightly understood, the mystical paths of India are not flight from the world but an attainment of the Real, which is finally discovered in its "only" reality when it is perceived in its real unity. The mystical union with this One does not put an end to the never-ending sparkle of innumerable forms on its surface, or suppress the alternation of pleasure and pain on the skin, but shows them in their reality, signs which both veil and reveal the one Presence and constantly recurring opportunities to experience the joy of union in it.

Naturally a thesis of this sort will send the case straight back to the tribunal of Western logic-choppers.[1] What about history? Every time the Eastern, and in particular the Indian, view of man comes anywhere near challenging our own, we invariably fall back on the comfortable cliché of the "anti-historicism" of the Indian vision of things, with its gloomy prediction of all the allegedly disastrous consequences it must bring for the adaptation demanded today to the climate of thought and rhythm of development imposed on the world by the frantic competition of the world powers.

For a clear view of the way in which Indian tradition sees man's place in time we must go back to the myths about the origin of the world composed in the archaic period by the inspired poets of the Veda. What the specialist in comparative religion finds remarkable is that it has been possible, within a single collection of canonical texts, for so many structurally irreconcilable origin myths to be placed side by side without difficulty and to form an authority as a whole.[2]

Each origin myth tells in its own way how the many came from the one and how time, the creator and destroyer, keeps souls and worlds moving in an endless circle, broken only by periods of latency during which the great creature which is the

[1] Raymond Panikkar, "The Law of Karman and the Historical Dimension of Man", *Phil. East and West* (1972), pp. 25-43.

[2] This pluralism has been a characteristic of the whole history of Indian thought. Six *darśanas*, each offering a philosophically structured vision of the real but all different both in their basis and their aim, have coexisted peacefully within Brahman orthodoxy as authorized interpretations of the message of the revealed writings.

All sleeps dreamlessly on the still waters of infinite substance from which everything will one day rise again.

The peaceful coexistence of so many mythical aetiologies must have a meaning. There are many indications which confirm the view that Indian thought has always been haunted by the problem of existence in time. It is characteristic that it is not satisfied with any particular way of formulating the problem. This rule has, as far as I know, only two exceptions and, on examination, they too support it. Moreover, these two exceptions are connected dialectically and historically. One is the Buddhist vision, the other is Śankara's *advaita*. What makes these exceptional is that they abandon mythical aetiology in favour of a position which is in intention radically demythologizing and demystifying. Not that a critical intention is in any way absent from the other systems of thought which have grown up in India—it can even be traced in the delicate working of the most archaic of the origin myths. These, however, are hardly radical. Their authors were unable or unwilling to give up all reliance on the mythical mode. In intention at least, things are different in our two exceptions.

But when we examine them, what do we learn about the spirit of eternal India from their deliberate and powerful originality? Gautama and Śankara had no intention of providing either the soothing glow of a complete rational solution for the philosophical mind haunted by the enigma of existence in time or the firm hope of a place of eternal rest for the religious mind contemplating in terror the mystery of life and death, even if their teaching has been often interpreted in this way. What they wanted to convey to whoever would listen is their conviction of the unimportance of the problem itself in both religion and philosophy. Philosophy and religion are finally placed back to back, not in the name of a libertine scepticism (a tendency resolutely opposed by both these thinkers), but in order to combine in an order of reality going beyond them both the truth postulated by the fact of empirical awareness and the truth postulated by the fact of the desire to go beyond it.

The message of these thinkers must therefore be read at a meta-philosophical and meta-religious level if we are to do it justice. What they proclaim is about the one and the many, time and eternity, but in a totally different context from the origin myths or the more or less erudite cosmologies and cosmogonies. Isolating in a pure state an original element of the Indian mind which can be traced from the beginning of the history of Indian thought, Gautama and Śankara concentrate the full weight of attention and intention on the goal not only of all speculation but also of all action, peace, a peace which quenches all thirst by cutting off desire at the root. More radically and more concentratedly than any other Indian thinkers, these two wanted to quench the flame of desire which springs from contact with phenomena when, thinking we have grasped them, we allow ourselves to be victims of their deceptiveness. Their aim was liberation from the chains of ignorance and concupiscence, dissipation of the ignorance about the operation of concupiscence. On this point Buddha expressed himself in a way more directly dominated by practice, Śankara in a way more in conformity with the traditions of philosophic thought. Both, however, left behind the theoretical question of the one and the many, time and eternity. In this way they realized the most secret and also the most tormenting desire of the whole history of Indian culture, to be totally and wholly in the world, in a state of constant rebirth, and so never growing old, in which the mind no longer succumbs to the age which begins to cloud it with the overcoming of the first frustration and never ceases to burden it more heavily with the accumulated weight of repeated frustrations.

The undeniable aspiration of India, and of the whole of the East with her, is clearly eternal life. On examination, we find that this is what both Taoists and Confucians, Hindus and Buddhists want. It is what the old Indian *rāja* in the legend wanted, who had the dying weighed before death and their bodies after death in order to discover if it might somehow be possible to catch the principle of life at the moment of its departure. Only in this context can we give a correct interpretation of the dogma common to almost all Eastern anthropologies, the doctrine of *karma*, so often misleadingly translated for Western use as the doctrine of transmigration or metempsychosis, as though its main point was to attribute everlasting existence to the individual soul under a succession of disguises.

The vision of the world and man summed up in *karma* has a quite different meaning. It holds out to the imagination a model for interpreting existence which is based on a principle which simultaneously dominates and co-ordinates all levels of its operation, anthropology, sociology, cosmology, ethics and religion, the principle of the primacy of intention over all other powers. The quickest way to explain this is perhaps to mention that in Indian thought it is the intention of killing which is the cause of the crime, and not the murder weapon, the fatal stroke or the conjunction of hazardous circumstances. In addition, in the logic of this approach, the intention of killing transforms the murderer no less than his victim, perhaps more. If the victim died a violent death, the cause must be looked for in his past. For the murderer, on the other hand, the crime will bear fruit in the future. Effective on the empirical level, the murderous intention none the less has no meaning on the level of the absolute. The death of the victim does not really put a stop to the continuance of his career. The circumstances of a new empirical existence will inevitably place him one day in a position to take vengeance on his murderer. The latter's action is the result of his practical ignorance of the way in which intentions motivated by the passions work themselves out to the detriment of their subject. On the details of the mechanism of retribution the opinions of teachers vary, but all are agreed in regarding it as ultimately inexorable. This is the core of the message which the doctrines of *karma*, different in detail but united in intention, compete with one another in expressing: intentions take shape and bear fruit because of ignorance.

Eternal life, which we saw earlier to be the aim of all the explorations of Indian thought, is understood in this context on the model of an existence empty of all karmic content and by that same fact removed from the vicissitudes of *Samsāra*. *Samsāra* denotes the total flux of existing beings, carried in the cosmic current because of the residual deposits of intentional acts which limit their experience to an individual sequence, given a particular tone by being placed in favourable or unfavourable situations, such as by birth into a determined caste. These individual series are not interrupted by empirical death, which therefore has no more than incidental value, a feature which is moreover in harmony with a vision of the universe which admits no beginning and no absolute end to the succession of worlds.

The ultimate term is of a quite different nature. Denoted by the words *moska* (deliverance) and *nirvāna* (vanishing), it escapes by its essence from any positive definition. The state to which it refers is best symbolized by empty space (*ākāśa*), which not only enables each thing to exist separately, but constantly penetrates them, precedes them in existence, remains identical with itself throughout their transformations and retains its identity after their disappearance. It is nevertheless a void which has positive value, and everything which has value proceeds from it by subtraction rather than by the addition of characters. Purging the intention of any trace of concupiscence, of any desire for profit, still does not on its own cancel out the speed acquired from the series of *karma*, but brings about deliverance by restoring to the mind, thus purified by *gnosis*, the ability to see through the deceptive glitter of phenomena and states of consciousness the omnipresence of the beatific void and to participate in it. There may be nothing in common, no metaphysical or logical point of contact between the empirical and the absolute, but, according to Indian wisdom, the possibility nevertheless exists of uniting them in a single spiritual experience which combines, beyond being and non-being, a principle which precedes them and which alone has the property of not frustrating those who have learnt (not) to desire it. This most paradoxical of intentions, a wanting which is a not-wanting, must be based on the double pillar of becoming aware of the meaning of the flux of existences (*samsāra*) and the simultaneous realization, in the same movement, of the wisdom which reveals the void undisturbed by the vicissitudes of their impetuous course (*jñāna*).

The corollaries of this conception of the final end are innumerable for those who can read the cultural facts of India in its light. It explains, for example, the absence of a sense of sin as it is known in monotheisms which hold a doctrine of creation.[3] No contrition is necessary in a world made up ultimately of pure intentionalities. If there is in one sense still room for a "conversion" (to saving *gnosis*), there is none for regret of a

---

[3] The Sanskrit word *pāpam*, generally translated "sin", stands for transgression of caste obligations, which are the way in which a particular individual makes his acceptance of *dharma*, the cosmic order or natural law.

fault, for a bad conscience, and still less for a contrite heart. In any case, nothing is ever definitively or irreversibly done wrong. Every intention bears its fruit, but once the fruit has been eaten the act has no further consequence. The situations which present themselves in the course of an existence all have a moral content. To submit to them without rebelling against the inexorable law of *karma* which manifests itself in them has in itself cathartic value. The same is true of the taboos imposed by the caste into which one is born and of all the other rules of conduct which follow the believing Hindu throughout his life, from conception to death. On the other hand, breathing "well" is enough to reduce the weight of *karma* at each breath. Keeping the rules of dietary purity has the same effect. In general, observance of *dharma*, which is intended to bring the individual and society into unison with the rhythm of life of the universe, contributes to bringing one closer to the threshold at which liberating access to saving knowledge becomes possible. But if the chances of salvation are improved in this way, they are still no more than chances, and the decisive step still has to be taken. It is also permissible to speed this upward movement by appropriate acts of asceticism, which systematically remove the harmful traces of past actions.

It is nevertheless possible, with a little trouble, to find within the immense spiritual treasury of Indian tradition expressions of repentance which have a "Christian" ring. At each step, however, one is brought to realize the marginal place of such expressions in relation to the broad currents which carry them along. There is one exception, the current of *bhakti*, which is the nearest to monotheism, the most devout and the most emotional of the spiritual currents of India, but even in this case the omnipresence of karmic determinism to every Indian consciousness leaves its characteristic mark on the experience of the fault which offends the Lord.

Another corollary is that social groups (family, *jati*, caste, relations of business or friendship, down to relations with domestic animals) are never formed only by chance, genes, economics or temperamental affinities. These groups of beings in fact sanction the karmic past of each of their members, which encourages the assumption—common in the East—that the same individuals have already lived in a group during past existences and will be together again in future reincarnations. The permanent bond between them is the whole mass of past intentional acts, the consequences of which weave themselves into a plait of contiguous tresses constantly lengthened by the new intentional acts which arise among the same subjects. This attitude to the group naturally gives a very particular emotional flavour to any social changes. Groups are like "constellations", travelling together through the ages of the world. Their solidarity for better and for worse is written on the indelible memory of the great-machine-for-the-retribution-with-justice-of-good-and-evil which is the universe, which is thought of in this respect as divided into many levels of retribution (heavens and hells).

This solidarity in space is of course only a particular case of the great total solidarity of all living things within *samsāra*. The precept of non-violence (*ahimsā*), that is, respect for the lives of all living things, is also a direct corollary of the karmic vision of the world as the place in which living creatures imprisoned in ignorance live a common destiny. Among all the possible levels of existence the earthly level nevertheless occupies a special place. It is recognized as the best place for the rapid consumption of karmic fruits and consequently as the best springboard for the leap towards deliverance. Deliberately to cut short the length of an earthly life before maturity is therefore the act, beyond all others, which will burden its author with the heaviest karmic debt.

The image of man formed by a culture is not only, and perhaps not primarily, a function of the action of dominant ideas on cognitive and evolutionary faculties or on the relations between ethics and cosmology, although they certainly affect its features. We can only note in passing the Machiavellian cynicism which emerges from many pages of the Arthashastra, whose importance for the analysis of human relations in Indian society has been rightly emphasized by the Indian Marxist W. Ruben.[4] This cynicism cannot be explained either by a theory of knowledge of the Indian type or by the doctrine of *karma*, and its origins should almost certainly be looked for more in the economic and social structures of ancient India. We cannot, however, end this

[4] *Das Pancatantra und seine Morallehre* (Berlin, 1959).

article without a mention of what is to be learnt from those ideal types offered for man's conduct, the anthropomorphic divinities, and among those by far the most important the Vishnuite avatars Kriṣna and Rāmā. Introduced by epics, which means in an originally "knightly" cultural context, but gradually Brahman-ized, they have a predecessor in the history of Vishnuism in the person of Nārāyana. His name means "man's younger brother". He cannot be separated from the mystical figure who appears in the Vedic hymn called the *Puruṣaśukta*, the Giant Man a quarter of whom is the universe, which he transcends with three-quarters of his being. The universe which grew out of the quarter of the Man itself also has the form of a man.[5]

Once the step was taken which in India leads from this "Man" to the "historical" avatars of epic—and there is not the slightest doubt that it was taken as early as the second century B.C.—Brah-man speculations, perhaps influenced by Hellenistic thought but certainly dedicated to the task of assimilating trends of popular devotion which were probably pre-Aryan to the Vedic tradition, took the path of a "gnosticism" which was to have great success throughout South-East Asia. The consequences of these develop-ments for the religious sense in Asia were to be no less important than, for example, those of Origen's commentary on the Song of Solomon in the Christian West. Like the latter, they linked gnostic and anthropological speculation to mystical analogy.

The speculations of the Upanishads on *ātman* (eighth century B.C.) and those of the Sānkhya on *puruṣa* (fifth century B.C.) cannot be considered apart from the direction taken in ancient Buddhism by the development of the doctrine of *anātta* (the absence of ulti-mate consistency in empirical creatures and things). The common background of these doctrinal developments is the conviction,

[5] Such a scheme of thought inevitably recalls the hierarchy of cosmic principles as found articulated in middle Platonism by Numenius of Apamaea, Philo of Alexandria, in many gnostic systems and in Origen. Beneath a first principle, which is transcendent (naturally in a more for-mally philosophical sense than that of the hymn of the Veda), appears a second principle, like the first, which is regarded as the more immediate cause of the forms of the empirical universe, which is imagined as a huge creature animated by the Soul of the world. This Soul is nothing other than the more or less degraded image of the "second god", who has the form of "Intellect" and as such is the archetype of the spiritual man im-prisoned in each of us by the man of mud.

which may have been the result of experiments in Yoga with states of awareness, that the life of common empirical experience split up into "moments" is in reality an "inauthentic" life and that doctrines and practices of spiritual training produced dissipation without profit. Since the experience of ecstasy was beyond the "subject-objective world" opposition, it seemed logical to assume the presence both at the heart of and beyond the empirical subject of a more fundamental participation in a meta-empirical transpersonal "reality" which was "present-absent" to all conscious activities and the antithesis of the "unhappy consciousness" at the mercy of the inconsistency of the perpetual flux of moments lived by the desire-consciousness.

The dam built by this form of speculation against the pressure of naïvely personalist sentiments reached its peak in Buddhism, around the period of the formation of the Great Vehicle. At no moment, however, was it ever high enough to prevent traces of "personalist" devotion (*bhakti*) from reaching the heart of the doctrinal sanctuary. And conversely, too, no devotional tendency which has grown up in India or been influenced by the Indian tradition can now ever completely ignore the set of problems centred on the topic of the impermanence of existence in *sam-sāra* which were forcefully introduced by Indian thinkers some centuries before Christ. It is in this "ultimate" context that we must understand the remarkable "openness" (in the sense of indefinableness) both vertically and horizontally of Eastern views of man. Without the light of this dimension the specificity of the phenomenon of man is blurred.

This fact is not without consequences for the quality of interpersonal relations, which are felt more as the just consequences of the inexorable law of *karma* than as a privileged opportunity of release from it. Liberation instead is regarded as the product of an "isolation" which is nevertheless as wide as—if not wider than—the whole universe and deeper than infinite space. The least bad description of its indescribable fullness is the metaphor of total emptiness.

Translated by Francis McDonagh

Alphonse de Waelhens

Some Aspects of the Psychoanalytical Image of Man

FREUD reminds us that during its history mankind has sustained or inflicted on itself three major narcissistic wounds. Copernicus deprived mankind of the dignity of being at the centre of the universe. Darwin located the human species in the continuity of a purely animal descent, thus assailing its "privileged" origin. And Freud with his discovery of the unconscious cancelled the primacy of a reason and consciousness supposed until then—at least in law—to be wholly in control of themselves.

Perhaps one might justly claim that this last achievement was the most fiercely resented (and most strongly resisted) of the three. Perhaps this seems doubtful in view of the present success [i.e., in the French-speaking world] of psychoanalysis and the universal interest that it awakens. But the claim is justified. Nearly a century passed before this recognition came—a century in which mankind underwent the most profound and rapid changes; moreover, it is arguable that much of the present discussion of psychoanalysis is consciously or unconsciously designed to "make it over" for various other purposes alien to its essential nature—here Marcuse and Deleuze are under the same heading as American culturalism and "adaptationism".

It is precisely the "narcissistic wound" attributed by Freud to modern man that the above-mentioned tendencies are bent on curing and effacing. It is far too simplistic to imagine that Freud's work is accepted as soon as one follows him in acknowledging a certain primacy of the unconscious, and the invalidity of the rationalist view of man. The mere fact that the latter is cheerfully given up as lost does not mean that satisfaction and happiness are henceforth to be sought *elsewhere* than in the impossible realm of an all-powerful reason. In fact, it was man's *vocation* to happiness that Freud made essentially questionable. From this viewpoint, it must be firmly maintained that an acknowledgment of the death wish is not, in Freud's work, the outcome of some accident, ineptitude, a revolution occasioned from without, or rogue speculation. It gives Freud's works that deep and ultimate meaning they had always, in essence, required. This is not the place to prove this point with an exegesis of Freudian texts. I think it is more to the point if I recall some of the metapsychological foundations of Freud's thought.

The human condition is decisively marked by the state of immaturity into which a human individual is born—an immaturity without equal in any other higher animal species. In ordaining that the new-born child pass from a situation of osmotic adaptation to one of almost complete non-adaptation, birth condemns the new being to difficulty and parasitism. No less does it condemn the individual (even though—to use Freud's own term—*nachträglich*, subsequently) to nostalgia for a mythic fullness which always existed and yet is now for ever inaccessible. In this sense, to be or to become a human being is to learn to renounce. Training in renunciation develops throughout a series of crises, each of which has for the subject individual, if successfully negotiated, a structuring function, which on each occasion gives renunciation a new dimension and meaning, but whose eventual frustration will inevitably bring in its wake the most severe pathological consequences. I shall now attempt a short analysis of the significance of each of these crises.

The Weaning Crisis

It is a question here, not of the vicissitudes of an historic and contingent event, but of a situation of structural implications, through which, in one way or another, every human individual, *because he or she is human*, has to pass. The weaning crisis poses to the future human subject the "question" of separation, isolation, severance and existence in a mode of deprivation. In this sense, weaning is only a term to characterize a process[1] that be-

[1] I am not confusing a situation of structural relevance and a process. The process is that which leads to the establishment of the situation.

gins at birth. The answer is a long time in coming, and in its oscillation between Yes and No, acceptance and rebellion, is in most cases marked by a certain ambiguity, even though—eventually—acceptance outweighs rejection. The renunciation of the mother's breast, a more or less successful event, confirms the *possibility* of obtaining a body which will be recognized, consciously or unconsciously, as distinct from that of the mother and other than it. The schizophrenic individual fails to cross this divide, but even in the non-psychotic, it is exceptional if this renunciation does not leave a few dark and shadowy areas, repressed in the unconscious, which can reappear under the form of symptoms—among which the anorexias and toxicomanias are both the most pronounced and serious.[2] A noticeable feature—in extreme cases—is the purely destructive nature of these symptoms: the refusal of food and active intoxication are symbolically—and in really extreme cases actually—equivalent to a non-violent suicide. At a less pathological level, a certain conscious or unconscious ambivalence of feelings towards the mother can disclose a survival of the same conflict. The unconscious is well aware that every mother, however perfect she was, necessarily and gravely deceived the child she bore.

This first stage opens the way for other crises. At the level I have just described, the "subject" is still without any feeling of his own unity. The deficiencies of his neurological equipment, the instability of his equilibrium and bodily position in space (each variation in which transforms what is offered for the individual's expression), the non-co-ordination of his movements (which deprives him of mastery of his body), the ingestion of nourishment and the process of natural elimination, give him the experience of a body which later on will seem to him divided in contradistinction to the unity acquired. But where is he to find that unity, if he has no means of acquiring it himself?

Lacan offers a major elucidation of this important point. Of course the mirror stage was known to psychologists[3] before psychoanalysts seized on it, but Lacan's interpretation essentially transforms its import.

---

[2] Clearly these, like all symptoms, can be determined: i.e., also express other conflicts.
[3] Wallon was the first to emphasize the full importance.

It is in a mirror that the individual has the first experience of his unity. This imaginary unity is just as much the object of a massive libidinal investment, encouraged by the support and interest originating in the mother. Yet, for the human subject, this gift, however narcissistic it may be, comes to mean preferment as much as a trap. Of course he acquires therein a valuable accession of his own unity. But this unity is offered to him in the imaginal form of an enticement; it is also that of *another* (even though he is also the *same one*), since the subject does not truly coincide with it.

One might call it suicidal in the sense that the subject learns of it that that which is the most "him" is also *elsewhere* and *other*, being quite distinct in its precise identity. Here we touch on that connection which indissolubly unites narcissistic love of self to a mortal aggressivity. Why? The subject is enticed and "tantalized" by his mirror image, and tries to reduce the distance between them. But, as the myth of Narcissus has warned us since time immemorial, he can do so only by destroying one or the other of the two terms, which immediately involves the destruction of the privileged term. There is no difference between aggressor and victim; one cannot even see who deals and who receives the blow. That is not all. In fact, the mirror-like nature of the first self-perception has even more serious consequences. It is responsible for the quasi-uncontrollable tendency which will drive the subject to live, imagine and "think" himself while *reifying* himself. Here there is no answer—and above all no definitive answer—to the question *What am I, Who am I?*

Or, rather, the truth of this question is its perpetual putting-in-question. But it is this that the subject, deceived by the quasi-mythic and narcissistic value ascribed to his mirror image, will obstinately try to evade. And he will never stop trying to attract the other into the game. If he does not succeed in "feeling at home in his own skin" (and how could he, since in this sense he has no "skin"?) he will look for the other's surety for this fake "skin", and he will use all his seductive tricks to persuade the other, of himself, to give him back that image which he more or less secretly suspects (which he cannot but suspect), so that—in the place of the other—it may become true and authentic. Then the cycle of dependence is complete. That this is more than a mere fable is best shown in the initial and naïve motives of most of those undergoing psychoanalysis. They are not very sure what they are, and the analyst, whose profession it is and who "knows", will show them once and for all. One might add, with almost no exaggeration, that the analysis comes to an end once the individual concerned accepts—and accepts fully—that he has to renounce this hope, see its meaninglessness, and not search anywhere else for a graven image of himself.

To return to the main theme. Henceforth the future subject, already identified with himself, but with a self which is just as much same and other, must recognize an other who is no longer himself. Here again psychoanalysis and child psychology agree in suggesting that first of all the infant unconsciously treats his actual like as a version of his mirror image.[4] How can he be dissuaded from this? By experiencing that dissymmetry which fatally intervenes in his relationship with that like, in contradistinction to what took place in regard to the likeness or mirror image, where the symmetry is never broken. The other takes a larger slice of the cake one hasn't taken oneself; or the other pockets the ball one thought to throw to oneself. That is a decisive turning-point in the experience of reality. We can understand it better by studying paranoia, which is no more than the frustration of this change. For the paranoiac the other is never more than an unconscious good or bad double of himself—but more often a loathsome one, since he projects on this double, in accordance with a series of mechanisms described by Freud in his interpretation of the Schreber case (1912), those among his own desires and tendencies which he cannot, or dare not, admit to himself. Consequently he is entitled to protect himself by any means from this double. This is the history of the persecutor or persecuted, or the Hitler image (without any suggestion that this character has to be explained in paranoiac categories) who, in *Mein Kampf*, accused the Jews of all the crimes that, later, he committed against them.[5]

[4] That is why it is absurd to think that a young child, which imputes to another what it has done itself, can be put forward as an example of "bad faith".

[5] I am aware that a few pundits opine that Hitler's natural father was probably Jewish, and that secretly and on some pretext Hitler had the village and the cemetery where his father was buried razed to the ground.

In the normal individual, on the other hand, the recognition of dissymmetry is "accepted", which introduces him to competition, emulation and rivalry as well as to sympathy and jealousy. Yet it is in relation to the mother's affection that this intrusion[6] of the other (therein become an other) is recognized.

This is not the last test. Even though it reveals to the subject the other who is not the same, this other is no less absolutely the same as he himself is. In other words, the intrusion complex does not locate the subject in regard to the difference of sexes, and the investment enjoyed by the other remains largely narcissistic since it relates to the like. In addition, the plurality accepted in the process is a factual plurality, which confers no right on anyone else.

The case of the Oedipus relationship is quite different. This leads the subject to invest the other of the opposite sex. In actual life, this other is normally, for the boy, the object that the subject's past calls to his attention: that is, his mother.[7] But—fatally —this claim involves rivalry in regard to the father, a rivalry which the subject soon discovers is dangerously insupportable, all the more since, in normal cases, he receives no encouragement from the object to engage in its conquest. The "castration complex", which effaces Oedipal love, is not primarily, as is often suggested (and as Freud sometimes asserted), the consequence of a real or imaginary threat: the castration is essentially symbolic. It is only a revival and restoration (in accordance with the meaning of the crisis presently being negotiated) of the renunciation which terminated each of the preceding crises.

It would be wholly wrong to think, on the basis of a necessarily summary account, that the Oedipal crisis has a purely negative significance. The contrary is true. The fact that the object escapes the desire and hope of the subject reveals in the object an autonomy and consistency which it did not then possess in the eyes of the same subject. That which is (imprecisely) known as

[6] Like the theory of the mirror stage, that of the intrusion complex (linked with the former) is the work of J. Lacan.

[7] Things are more complicated for the girl. She does not discover her Oedipal object in the extension of pre-Oedipal relations. The deception of being born without a penis detaches the girl from her mother. She imputes the deprivation to the mother and this persuades her to turn against the penis-bearer—the father.

the pre-Oedipal *object* is for the corresponding subject no more than the obligatory and more or less willing boundary of his tendencies. As far as the subject experiences it, it has no independence or being-in-itself, and the relations to which it gives rise are characterized by their insidious violence and deep-seated versatility. The pre-Oedipal "object" is something to be consumed. It is not included in the actuality of adult experience, but is wholly marked by a more or less thwarted *wishful thinking*. The frustration of the Oedipal claim teaches the subject that, as it were, the object has its lines to speak and its part in the play. Or (and how many alleged adults have never succeeded in recognizing this *truly*) that loving and being loved are in no way synonymous, or necessarily reciprocal. Without such an experience and disappointment, the subject cannot acquire a *full sense* of reality, of its density and stability, ineluctably marked by what Bachelard (and Sartre subsequently) called the coefficient of adversity of things. This is why he will himself become capable of stable investments and highly-nuanced and tender feelings, whose depth will no longer be confused with mere eruptive violence.

But, above all, the liquidation of the Oedipus complex introduces the subject to the Law. By accepting the prohibition of incest, the forbidden orientation to the mother, the subject receives in return the fullness of his identity. A humanity given up to adventitious copulation would also be a humanity where no one could any longer locate himself in the sequence of generations, and where there would therefore no longer be any true and complete identity. Here we can agree with Lévi-Strauss that the prohibition of incest defines the transition from nature to culture.

The effacement of the Oedipus complex is therefore correlative to the establishment of a pact. In exchange for the renunciation of the subject, the father confers a name in which both pledge their word. Here again, there is more symbolism than factuality; this is clear from a strange paradox: the name I bear is not actually my own unless I am not the only one to bear it, unless my father bore it before me. But the same is true for this father, for my grandfather, and so on. The father who bestows the name is therefore a symbolic father, much more than the individual of flesh and blood who was my actual progenitor.

*   *   *   *

The structures which I have just described so summarily are universal in that they define crises and complexes (or, if a more existential terminology is preferred, *questions*) on which the edification of any human subjectivity depends. However, the way in which each of these structures establishes itself in the coming-to-be of each individual subject is *historical*, and dependent on the past, whether real or imaginary, of that same subject. The difficulties which have marked them, the fantasies which accompanied and incised them, the setbacks or semi-setbacks by which they were resolved, have been repressed. This does not mean that they are inactive, since in as much as they interpret or are connected to aspirations, to disappointed or unacknowledged desires of the subject, they tend to reappear under some disguise in the subject's actual further life in order to obtain there some satisfaction through compromise. But under this disguise they remain locatable in and by the subject's language (it being taken for granted that behaviour also "speaks"); and the psychoanalytic dialogue, under the conditions and with the methods proper to it, can then reveal them to the subject.

There is no space here to go into these infinitely complicated questions. I mention them only in order to pose problems appropriate to the theme of this issue of *Concilium*.

There can be no doubt that psychoanalytic practice and theory considerably qualify the self-image (or, rather, images) that humanity has traditionally put forward. But they do not make all humanism a vain enterprise. Even if Freud was, as has been said, a "master of suspicion", he was so only in order to show us the truth: the truth about mankind, or at least a part of it. In this respect, psychoanalysis is openly opposed to the anti-humanism and anti-formalism of certain humane sciences today, for which a human truth is a meaningless notion. When Freud harshly denounces certain illusions, and in particular those of rationalist optimism, he does so in order to estimate the real chances for reason. He repeated more than once that, however weak they might be, they were nevertheless our only valid hope. This reasonable reason knows its term and that it will not afford the kind of happiness of which our narcissism never ceases to dream. It knows that it must guide rather than impose. It does not and never will use force. It does not deny that man can change himself, and even less that above all he must accept himself as he is. But this margin of actual mutation is minute, and effective only in so far as man heeds his truth. Yet it ought to be aware that this concern for truth is only one dimension of man and that there are others, not at all the most deprived, by whom man, whether he wants it or not, seeks only to abuse himself. He does so primarily by pursuing satisfactions which he thinks he desires for themselves when they are only the mask or substitutes for others, which he does not know or cannot acknowledge. The example of the lover's choice needs no comment here.

But it is no less self-delusive, and no less dangerous, to imagine that man can kill all his desire and aggressivity. Some excesses of asceticism, devotion, sacrifice, and some apologies for self-offering, are only camouflaged aggressions; they are all the more intense for their lack of self-awareness.

In conclusion, I should like to quote Antoine Vergote: "Freud identified the consciousness as the location of error as much as of truth. The cunning spirit whose guile Descartes so feared is within man himself: in the demoniac power of his unconscious. Freud exorcized it in calling it by its name. He recognized that the core of man is not the spirit, but instinct and desire. He demonstrated the exchanges between the archaeological language of the symbolic body and the discourse of reason. He denounced the illusions of the voluntarist language of the ego. His impression of freedom, the force of his will, his aspiration to mastery, are also to a large extent instinctive impulses. Freud reminds man, who thinks he is an active and creative power, of the unsuspected burden of his past."[8]

Obviously, it would be too easy, and erroneous, to imagine a reference to psychoanalysis to be enough to constitute a philosophic anthropology. There is still a discursive reason, a reflective power of conscience, and a creative liberty of man. Psychoanalysis shows that they cannot be examined apart from their essential roots in the instincts.

Translated by John Griffiths

---

[8] W. Huber, H. Piron, A. Vergote, *La psychanalyse, science de l'homme*, pp. 192–3.

Gérard Granel

The Obliteration of the Subject
in Contemporary Philosophy

IT SEEMS appropriate here to define "contemporary philosophy" as a number of texts answering to the following criteria:

(*a*) the period to which they are co-temporary is the terminal period of metaphysics;

(*b*) philosophy no longer "contains" them but, on the contrary, is contained in them;

(*c*) philosophy, however, continues to serve them as an eponym, even though there is no question here of "negligent" categorization, or of that alleged (though in fact non-existent) situation in which "words fail us";

(*d*) their greater generality in relation to the philosophic order of discourse is the same phenomenon as their location in a determinateness of practice; and the same as the radical critique of an alleged sphere of generality in which there is an autogenetic, local specification of a unique "logos" (none other than the metaphysical dream);

(*e*) this practical restriction, or materiality of multi-determinate discourse, nevertheless occurs as a "displacement", or as a "recurrence", of the mere positive data in their mere horizon of positivity (whatever the capacity of a text of "contemporary philosophy" may be to question and thematize this alien dose of unreality in it).

There are more texts answering to these restrictive criteria than their rigour might lead one to suppose. Above all, they disallow as "contemporary philosophy" anything which is even redolent of phenomenology, Marxism, structuralism, and so on; for these put their trust in whatever degree of "actuality" there may be in their "theses", and remain blind to the metaphysical operation of their very composition. They also rule out all doctrinal attempts (emanating from one traditional school or another) to "link up with" "contemporary data" or the "modern mind". They do not allow any confusion of a work of "contemporary philosophy" with a positive text in which there is a direct deposition (or a deposition in the unique mediative form of a science) of a specific praxis (linguistics, economics, mathematics, theatre, and so forth). But, in spite of all this clearance work, there are still several families of texts which constitute "contemporary philosophy"—a quite extensive literary production which is fairly difficult to classify.

The principle of an appropriately accurate classification may be found at the two limit-points that a contemporary text always unites: the point where it touches on metaphysical tradition, and that where it is grounded in the material determinateness of a specific practice.

The *de*construction of metaphysics is possible not only by way of one or other *thematic* threads, which would only result in a taxonomy of destructions, featuring as so many families of discourse those, for example, which are concerned with the death of God; those which reduce the "philosophy of language" to its linguistic vacuum; those which show up the "theory of knowledge" in all its epistemological indetermination; those which reduce the "philosophy of right" to bourgeois production; and so on. Each "author" and each "trend" is then defined by his or its manifestation of, and the more or less extensive dominance in it of, one or more of these "themes". Rather, much more decisively, it is made possible by attacking, irrespective of the themes, the *element* of metaphysical writing *as such*. The principle of differentiation of texts then becomes the degree of vigilance and of generality to which the destruction of metaphysics is taken—raised in this instance to its formal power; but, primarily, and before such an internal subsidiary order, it is the principle which differentiates from all other texts, those established expressly at this level of formality.

Metaphysics in general (therefore as much in its initial Greek version as in its medieval or its modern form) can be located, grasped and destroyed at the highest level of generality, which comprises the revelation of the dominance of Presence in the cancellation of Difference, and that of the onto-theo-logical constitution of discourse. If it is always, more precisely, a question of the specifically *modern* form of metaphysical destiny, then to tackle the element of metaphysical composition as such would mean attacking the "subject" as such, and therefore attacking subjectivity as constituting the modern form of the domination of presence. *The destruction of the subject is not one theme among others in contemporary philosophy, but that which defines and comprises it as constituting the task proper to it.*

This struggle takes place today in various forms: it may emanate (now we are at the other extreme which should govern a classification: the diversity of practices) from a still indeterminate reference to *practicity* as such; or it may arise from the "philosophic" revival of a specific practical field, of which there are four varieties: *text, desire, machine* and *production.*

The first confrontation is that undertaken by Heidegger in his *Sein und Zeit*: a dispersal of the element of subjectivity (taken by Husserl to its extreme), not in attacking merely the "thesis" of the subject, but in destroying the sense of being which first of all gives rise to this thesis, and to all those which result therefrom, and the language that they speak, the air that they breathe. It is a question of elucidating, in general, the tendency of the existent to manifest itself as "pragma for a praxis" *before* its reduction to the state of "thing for a representation", and *in opposition* to it. Hence there appears simultaneously the opposition of *Da-sein* as *In-der-Welt-sein* and that of "subjectivity" (subjectivity in the transcendental sense) in the form of worldlessness (*Weltlosigkeit*). This is the highest level of formality.

However, nothing is more uncertain, or more certainly false, than to wish to discover in this *general* revelation of practicity that very *genre* which would contain and unify as its *species* what I have more prudently called the four "varieties" of practical field: *text, desire, machine* and *production.* This would be to provide a "completion" and a systematic theoretical "unity"—as if under a speculative roof—for the works of "contemporary philosophy" which oppose subjectivity from the basis of each (or several) of these determinations of practice; but the will to systematic unity in a generality of being (which would forget the Aristotelian lesson that *this generality is not itself generic*) would also restore the metaphysical illusion of the elevation of philosophy to the status of science, and consequently the very element of subjectivity.

However, the question one would like to take part in asking at this point is that of the "connection" "between" the generality of Heideggerian procedure and the specificity of "real" processes which is the concern of other contemporary writings in the struggle against subjectivity.[1]

This seems necessary in order to try to understand in what and why these "real" processes are nevertheless those of "philosophic" writing, at least in the sense that it is obsessed by a certain "unreality". The concept of text, for example, only operates in opposition to the dominance of the subject on condition that it becomes, in such a written composition, that which it *is not* in regard to literature, rhetoric and "criticism"; and, if the text is considered now as that of a given language, only on the condition that the language is no longer that which it is for speaking subjects, or that which it is as an object of linguistic science. Not that it is a question of surveying all these "direct data" in order to escape "over there" (into the perigraphic security of an "interior" of "fundamental" onto-logic, auto-differentiated in as many areas as necessary), but because something should correspond to the "vague" nature of discourse in which the "data of experience" and the "precise findings of science" are re-immersed, recast, "strangely" recomposed, and treated as the broken components of a (re)collage which liberates (manufactures) with them

[1] One should really speak of a *struggle* and not, as in my title I imprudently engaged to do, of the *obliteration* of the subject—a term which could persuade some to think that the element of modern metaphysical writing fades or disappears of itself. In fact, here as elsewhere, there are two camps. The fact that *theoretical* practice is in question does not mean that contemporary philosophy has only, "serenely" or "objectively", to survey that which is, abandoning to the "truth of things" any concern to regulate its "debate" with Tradition. For it is a question of theoretical *practice*, which means that no thesis, no meaning and no ideality is separable from the materiality of its production, and that truth itself weaves itself, machines itself, desires itself, and produces itself, not in debate, but in struggle.

figures without existing models—ultimately a sort of Wonder-
land of the possible where "meaning" itself extends or shortens
itself; where that which does not speak speaks; and that which
speaks transforms itself into noise. This is a strange power for a
written work which, at the very moment of its so-called "vagueness", is by virtue of that very vagueness precise and controlled—
not by a concept, since all concepts arise and separate in its movement, but as a *working* which follows the apertures and resistance
points of a *material*.

Material, matter, here, is however, the Imaginary, that hollow
framework of all that is "real", and in a sense the rejection of
any datum or given, the stone of any object. But where do the
resourcefulness, limit and vitality of contemporary philosophic
efforts (work being the enemy of the subject, the irreconcilable
contrary of the "contemplation of the idea") come from? Where,
if it is necessary to refuse to *identify* it as *difference*, and therefore
as *the* Difference, is being "itself" as difference, being-in-differ-
ence? The fact that this generality is not a genre, that it does not
define interior, base, "original" (or ultimate) instance, is no reason
to ignore it. Not only because without it there would no longer
be any recognition that in philosophic labour "things" begin to
"tumble and dance", but because one would understand all the
less that they pass into one another, and, so to speak, "become"
the others, or make those others become them. Not only is a
machine in this metamorphosis not at all mechanical, and a text
a tissue once more: the *desiderium* no longer containing
desire in its lack; desire slaving without need; production,
tackling metaphysics and economics, transmutes them and reveals
them as the parts of rhetoric and (consequently) wrings their
neck. Not only that; the fabric, the machined stuff, the desired,
the product, much less dubiously than scents, colours and sounds,
"account for themselves". In imagination. But in imagination in
the sense that each takes its image (character, countenance) only
from such a "correspondence". In this meta-morphosis their
morpho-logy is (nervously) consolidated.

The question I asked just now, about a to-and-fro between a
generality without location and the repetition of specific practices, already has a precedent *within* one of these practices: production. Marx was in fact the first to confront this abrupt wall of

a generality without any genre, when, having seen that the critique of political economy could be assembled round the concept of production, he also perceived that this unity had no sphere or substance, and was to some extent devoid of any "reality"— since he always refused to accept any "production in general" or "general production".

In addition, Marxism is not defined or definable (no matter how) on the basis of the quadruple homonymia of practice, but only on the basis of the function of *pars totalis* enjoyed by one, and only one, of the four corners between which contemporary discourse is conducted, and, in the process of exchange, comes into being. Just as for Aristotle, *ousia* is the category which *indicates* (but will not say) unity where it and all others "are being"; similarly production is that index of Marxist unity which *must remain privileged*: that is, from which in one way or another one has to start or to which one has to return, in relation to other threads of discourse (equally "primary", or rather equally functioning and equally free, it would seem) than the text, machine and desire. If this were not so, Marxism would dissolve into the indeterminate space of "contemporary philosophy", and its historico-political efficacy would be removed (that is, it would be deprived of *everything*). Therefore it is necessary that the part shows (labours to show) that it is effectively the whole, and the discourse of production weaves all the others.

In fact the role of non-generic generality played by production in the entire work of Marx (indivisible, since it is precisely his youth [genesis] which remains immature in his maturity, or the silence of its division which assures its unity) either will not be understood (and Marx as a whole will then be held to be comprised in the content of his theses apart from "labour on the work" (which means: all unreadable Marx, apart from the ideological apparatus of state or party, apart from the congresses, learned societies, colloquia and the "confrontations with believers": a cultural pulp, a politician's nightmare which will be (is) political nothingness), or else will be deciphered only within the limits of the only text in which the struggle against metaphysics takes this generality of production into account: the *Economic and Philosophic Manuscripts of 1844*. But in this text it is not possible (in any case, it is no longer) *not* to perceive that the struggle with metaphysics, in accordance with the classical restriction of the "genealogical" writings, still occurs within, and wholly within, the element of modern metaphysics: that is, within "subjectivity", and in order to consolidate it.

Therefore the question is posed of knowing how—in the unity of the *work in progress*, that is, in the difference between (i.e., the non-indifference between) its maturity and its beginning, in the propagation of the silence of division—production rounds on subjectivity and reduces it to a still unnamable theoretical practice. If we do not pursue this prob'em to the end, the "historical" future of Marxism, confirming its former exhaustion, and on the contrary calling in question all its recent theoretical growth, will be only the "socialist" version of the future of the modern world, a version of a time which, being the time of the subject, is "already" *the* dead-time.

But the same will happen if the discourse of desire, the machine and the text, after having performed this (immense though *transitory*) service of having, by virtue of its *formal* equivalence with that of production, injected all the work of "contemporary philosophy" into the veins of paleo-Marxism (that of the meaningful content of the thesis directly *levied* on the writings of Marx and in "oblivion" of those writings), itself happened to "forget" that in these very writings production is not only a thesis, but in fact writes itself and all the rest: that is, all the thematic content and all the thetic (methodological or "doctrinal") attitudes: that is, what one speaks about or of how one speaks about it, and that which one says about it.

Hence it would seem, in this kind of picture of contemporary philosophy, whose motif is the "obliteration of the subject" as the common task of this philosophy, that we have to do with something rather like a workshop in which *several* tasks have been begun, but where there is no question of eradicating difference in bringing them to unity. However, unity cannot be abandoned; on the contrary, the concept has to be worked on, and all the more because it has already been worked on and conceived in a divided fashion as a question of Difference *and* as a question of production.

Surely the last question is wholly necessary: "Who will be the subject of this work?" If the head of the philosopher, like the cupola-heads of Dali, burst into the azure blue of an indifferent sky, if the "interior" is decidedly no more than a volume without work and without trace, a fine architecture without any use, henceforth ruined from above and abandoned to the clouds and the birds; in short, if there is no longer any subjectivity, then the question of real subjects arises: the *subjects* of a *task*.

This is to put the question on the wrong track and to develop it in terms of the kind of division of labour. Not that this form of question does not arise and go a long way. For example, it raises the impossibility of continuing much longer to teach philosophy in the institutional university following the model of the individual fragmentary imparting of instruction, where each teacher is the governor-owner of his discourse *because*—at least that is the justificatory ideological background—truth is the essence of the subject (transcendental, to be sure, but reactivable at least by right in any empirical subject, and all the more so the more qualified the subject is), or because knowledge is a function of consciousness. But however important it may be not to prevent oneself from being led towards such consequences, the question of the real subjects of labour, which the traditional evidence of the metaphysical subject reveals as soon as it itself disappears, the taste of the difficulty should take us more downstream, at the risk of no longer noticing the banks which could give the question a fairly recognizable contour. Hence:

—admitting that "philosophic" labour is not a labour of science, but a "hermeneutics of banality";

—admitting that the text which this *hermeneia* would decipher is no "analytics of subjectivity", but a collection of practices which, even though they are for each individual "mine every time", are no less a collective historical text, already multi-coded and overprinted.

Then the question of knowing in what sense collective-divided labour in some way passes through "me" supposes that the banality of which this ego is the ego should be understood as it is practised, that is, as an historical collective banality, and that, in consequence, the collectivity as such conceives itself and organizes itself as the real subject of philosophic labour.

This is what it does in any case, for the very possibility and all the realized forms of "philosophic activity" have always been subject to their *political* regulation. But the difficult point is not there. It is not even the problem of asking how this political control, instead of being the object of a general disclaimer (only liberal freedom conceiving itself as a "framework", and not as the real subject of a "scientific" work in which it pretends to "respect" the dignity which accrues to it from the fact that it is its own proper subject in its own right), would on the contrary be acknowledged, desired and expressly and publicly organized. The difficult thing is to know whether the political collectivity is even possible, just if it is possible, historially-historically, for a general unity of practice to come together as a people (or a community of peoples, or one humanity).

Certainly there is no need to wait for the question to be "treated" in order to work on it. But perhaps the time has come when it is no longer possible to work without the question even being posed, and more and more insistently. But, since it is impossible to see what a "general unity of practice" would mean (as a political, actual historical practical collective)—just as at least one no longer sees it (and one no longer wishes to see it) under the form in which the Christian faith, degenerating to "Christianity", long ago usurped—and fulfilled—this function. Perhaps the succession of the celestial metaphysical subject will never be ensured by mankind as the actual earthly subject, unless— and to the extent that—politics takes Difference as its "object" and "goal". Not, of course, expressly, as such and in its concept, but in practice and as obscurely as anyone likes.

Translated by V. Green

Alexandre Ganoczy

New Tasks in Christian Anthropology

NOWADAYS, hardly anyone still uses the lift of neo-scholastic anthropology, which functioned so smoothly for so many centuries between the storeys of cosmology and angelology.[1] Because of its fundamental dualism, in which body and soul, the natural and the supernatural and sin and grace were so sharply contrasted, it has become quite out of tune with modern man's understanding of himself and his world. For this reason, it can no longer communicate with contemporary anthropologies, which are distinguished by a scientific method and an empirical and positive way of thinking. On the one hand, neo-scholasticism, with its dichotomy between creation and grace, sees man and his world in a "mythological" light. On the other, contemporary structuralism[2] condemns the neo-scholastic anthropology as mythological because it makes use of Platonic and Aristotelian categories to qualify man as static, by taking only religious factors such as creation and redemption into account and not man's non-religious structures and practical functions. Neo-scholasticism has also been accused of being ineffectively abstract, on three main charges. The first is its use of a metaphysics of substance, which is quite unacceptable to contemporary philosophical thought.[3] The second is the neo-scholastic equation of its own system with

---

[1] L. Ott, *Grundriss der katholischen Dogmatik* (Freiburg, 1965), pp. 111–148.

[2] J. B. Fages, *Comprendre le structuralisme* (Paris, 1967), p. 41.

[3] H. Rombach, *Substanz, System, Struktur* (Freiburg and Munich, 1965/1966).

the human reality at a time when this reality is being system-atized in a much more concrete way by the natural and humane sciences. The third charge is that it is discredited as an ideology without what Marx has called "interests and passions" and as a theology which is too little concerned with the message and the praxis of faith.

On the other hand, the theologian who is trying to formulate the Christian understanding of man, and the world in the present situation performs two basic tasks. Firstly, he receives a contem-porary philosophical understanding of man's subjective existence and secondly he remains open to the questions posed by the natural and humane sciences. Thus he does not qualify sin as the loss of supernatural status, but takes human psychology, in this case man's consciousness of guilt, as his point of departure for a definition of sin.[4] It is hardly necessary to point out how radically this assimilation of modern philosophical anthropology has renewed the Christian view of man and how far it has re-moved it from neo-scholastic thought. The modern theologian has, on the other hand, not gone quite so far in his openness to the questions raised by the natural and humane sciences, although theological discussions about the problem of "hominization"[5] have given new life to the old doctrine of creation. The very fact that such discussions have even taken place shows how unsatis-factory the neo-scholastic arguments about the divine act of creation were.

One consequence of these two modern attitudes has, however, been the appearance of a certain panic among theologians. They have discovered that the natural and humane sciences are mainly concerned, not with persons, but with data and structures and that these sciences cannot be secondary to the alliance between modern philosophy and theology. The theologians' panic result-ing from the invasion of structuralism is not difficult to under-stand—they are sensitive to the danger that the study of man will become dehumanized and that man will become exclusively in-terested in objective facts. After all, it is certain that structuralism

[4] P. Schoonenberg, "Sin and Guilt", *Sacramentum Mundi*, VI, pp. 87–92.
[5] P. Overhage and K. Rahner, *Das Problem der Hominisation* (Freiburg, 1961).

not only places objectivity at a higher level than subjectivity and thus endangers the value of personal existence, but also questions the humanism which is indirectly at least based on man's relationship with God in Jesus Christ.

Can it, for example, be meaningful to speak nowadays of God's communication of himself being the bearer of man's becoming conscious of himself if all that modern man understands is the positive, empirical verification of certain facts? It would certainly seem as though the most urgent question today is that of speech and communication. Even the speech of renewed, existential Christian anthropology is stammering and almost incomprehensible when it is used in dialogue with the "foreign" language of structuralism and related sciences. Contemporary Christian anthropology is constantly failing in its task of maintaining a resolutely critical attitude because it is uncertain about its identity and has not yet found a suitable means of communicating with those with whom it has to take part in dialogue. In what follows, I shall try to analyse the problems involved in the tasks of affirming its identity and of becoming capable of communication—the two conditions that must be satisfied if the new Christian anthropology is effectively to criticize various current movements against humanism.

I. Identity

The only person who is capable of communication is the man who is completely conscious of his own identity and able to affirm it in the act of communication. This applies equally to Christian anthropology if it is not to give up communication in favour of irresolute adaptation and sacrifice itself to every new scientific system.

1. *The Specific Formal Object*

The task confronting Christian anthropology of affirming its identity cannot be carried out by clinging rigidly to traditional teaching. Certain aspects of Christian doctrine, such as monogenism as against polygenism, man's origin and original sin, or his immortal soul as the "form" of his body, have to be set aside so that the essentially Christian understanding of man and especially of his future can be adequately expressed in contemporary Christian language.

What is the formal object of this specifically Christian understanding of man? It corresponds to the structure or "form of organization" of the human reality which results from man's special relationship with God in Christ. In a word, the formal object of Christian anthropology is the consequence of Christo-theo-logy.

2. Openness to the World and to God in Christ

What is meant by this is discussed in another contribution to this journal. I shall therefore briefly outline the essence of this relationship which must underlie the identity which has to be affirmed by Christian anthropology—which is Christian in so far as it interprets man's openness to the world as openness to God in Christ. The empirical fact that man, unlike the animals, is constantly going beyond himself and his world is given a central point in God as the one who is beyond this world and over and against man in his individual and collective transcendence of himself. The anthropological importance of this is revealed, in Christianity as opposed to other religions, in the historical event of Christ. The God who revealed himself in Christ is over and against man, near and yet far, immanent and yet infinite and he offers man, in his openness to the world, an ultimate goal without defining its end.[6]

This is the specific formal object to which Christian anthropology must hold if it is to affirm its identity in confrontation with contemporary scientific and philosophical anthropologies and in which it will recognize and interpret the human predicament. This will also provide the Christian understanding of man with its own special structure. No one would deny that this Christian study of man was historically prior to and to some extent prepared the way for the modern secular anthropologies and that it is marked by freedom, historicity, constant questioning and a concern for the future—characteristics which are also

---

[6] W. Pannenberg deals in detail with this theme in his *Was ist der Mensch? Die Anthropologie der Gegenwart im Lichte der Theologie* (Göttingen, 4th edn., 1972), pp. 5-13.

found in a secular form in the anthropologies of Western scientists, Marxists, existentialists and atheists.

We are bound to draw attention here to the very serious danger to this formal object of Christian anthropology caused by the death of God theologians, with their enthusiastic reduction of God as transcendent, infinite and over and against man and of christology to a one-dimensional "Jesuology". It is impossible to speak in a Christian way about man without insisting on the God who has revealed himself in Jesus the Christ and who is over and against man and transcendent yet immanent. To reduce the reality of God to the level of man is to make it impossible to answer the obviously urgent contemporary question as to whether we can express, discuss or address God at all. Seen in this light, the formal object of Christian anthropology is above all marked by faith, but this should not stand in the way of scientific knowledge, since the religious relationships, of which faith is a special form, provide us with a reality that can be analysed. Historical, sociological, psychological and even psychosomatic research can be carried out into religion and faith as universal structural factors and into the aspects of the totality of man to which those factors belong. This in turn provides the arena in which communication can take place between Christian anthropology and other contemporary anthropologies.

II. Communication

1. The necessary *condition* of this dialogue between Christian and non-Christian anthropologies is that each partner is recognized as representing a legitimate hypothesis. It is difficult for purely scientific anthropologists to take the Christian view seriously, because of the stagnation in recent centuries of the neo-scholastic understanding of man.

(a) There are, however, certain indications that some of the achievements of recent scientific research into the biblical understanding of man are being accepted as valid by non-Christian anthropologists—for instance, the Old Testament insistence that man is one body-spirit and that he lives within a community and within history. Above all, these anthropologists have come to respect the modern historical and critical approach to exegesis.

(b) Biblical anthropology is also based on texts which are open to linguistic analysis and which contain statements made in an historical context which can be verified and understood as historically unique or as universal in meaning. This provides further opportunity for communication between Christian and purely scientific anthropologies. The importance of exact research into the New Testament texts, using philological methods and linguistic analysis, for a theological anthropology with a christological basis has been shown—in a negative way—by the failed or at the most only partly successful attempts to reconstruct the New Testament message in a purely "secular" form.[7]

2. Christian anthropologists have at the same time also to consider seriously the other anthropologies, especially in the spheres of biology, psychology, sociology and philosophy. Biology must be placed first on this list for good reasons. Since Roger Bacon's scientific investigation of nature in the Middle Ages,[8] biology has contributed enormously to man's understanding of himself and has enabled him to come to a more precise knowledge of his own position in the natural order and to make better use of nature. Darwin's theory of evolution, for instance, has given rise less to a fatalistic acceptance of determinism and more to a discovery of the biological value of the human reality. Certainly, biologists have come closer than anyone to an understanding of man in his concrete existence and there are many important points of contact between biology and the humane sciences.

(a) *Theology and Biology*

It would be wrong for Christian anthropology to ignore the present trend in biology and, for instance, to consider exclusively the findings of philosophy, because man's concrete existence does not begin at the level of free choice—its point of departure is his physiological condition. Human biology is the basis of all man's freedom, his openness to the world and to God and any possible

---

[7] See H. R. Holcomb's pertinent criticism of Paul van Buren's attempt in J. Lee Ice and John J. Carey (eds.), *Dass Gott auferstehe* (Zürich, 1971), pp. 66–84.

[8] See H. Grundmann, "Bacon", *Religion in Geschichte und Gegenwart* I (Tübingen), pp. 832 ff.

spiritual transcendence. Since freedom is dependent on biological determinism, biological knowledge is indispensable to our understanding of man. As Nietzsche discovered, man's affirmation of his existence is stimulated by this knowledge—conscious of his biological value, he will affirm his finite nature absolutely and commit himself to the struggle for his future.

This consciousness of his biological structure is clear from his full acceptance of the neo-Darwinian theory of evolution and the hope rather than fear that has resulted from the possibility of discovering scientifically his origins and thereby of becoming his own master.[9] Biological research into the origin of man has become part of his struggle for autonomy. His growing knowledge of his own origin is accepted as a factor in shaping and changing his existence, although this has unfortunately gone beyond the limits of manipulation.

Important contributions have been made to man's understanding of himself by biological research into forms and origins and by ethology. The study of morphology has confirmed that man's organs are unspecialized and that he is an "unfinished" being, both in the passive and in the active sense. It has shown that the individual is both conditioned by and dependent on society and that his physical organism is an ideal instrument for the spirit.[10] This absence of organic specialization enables man as an individual and in society to be open to the world, to shape it and to create a culture. The study of his origin has demonstrated that selection, mutation and domestication are essential features in the evolutionary process of hominization and have a decisive influence in modern man's consciousness of the need for change. Nothing can take place in his world without conflict, adaptation and separation—this is an accepted principle of the neo-Darwinian theory which has also powerfully influenced contemporary thinking. Finally, ethologists have pointed out that instinct and intelligence are closely related in animals and in man and that play and speech are essential to the self-fulfilment of both. This ethological evidence has given a new dimension to the

[9] See P. Overhage and K. Rahner, *op. cit.*, pp. 359 ff.
[10] F. Hartmann, "Anthropologie", *Religion in Geschichte und Gegenwart* I (Tübingen), pp. 404 ff.

humanities and to philosophy in their attempts to understand the human reality and has also provided total structures which have to be used by theologians in communication with other anthropologies.

Let me conclude this section by briefly suggesting possible points of departure for the way in which Christian anthropologists might include the results of a biological study of man in their investigations, without setting aside the formal object of the specifically Christian understanding of man. Firstly, the biological law of continuous evolution can be linked with the theological principle of man's individual and communal process of becoming himself. Secondly, man's sexuality and social character can be considered within a single biological and theological vision. Thirdly, gnosis and praxis can be seen to be closely related in the ethological sense—the ethical orientation of statements about faith in the Christian anthropological sense. Fourthly, language may be considered as an origin, as a self-fulfilment and as a factor in evolution or a biocatalyst—as God's word and man's answer in faith. Fifthly, struggle, competition and confrontation have to be recognized as a law of biological life and linked with the dialectics of the crucifixion as the law of life according to Christian faith.

(b) Theology and Psychology

There is much more communication between Christian anthropology and psychological anthropology than there is between the first and the much more fundamental biological understanding of man, perhaps because Freud has been more completely assimilated by theologians than Darwin. Like practical theology, neo-Freudian praxis is educative and healing and there are, especially in the United States, already strong links between them. Depth psychology has tended to replace philosophy in the Christian understanding of man, leading to a firm commitment to praxis. Christian anthropology has unfortunately come in this way to be threatened by a one-sided pragmatic emphasis, since this praxis tends to lose contact with the underlying theory and the specifically Christian formal object is then considered only in the foreground. There is therefore a real need for communication between Christian anthropology and psychology to be deepened and extended if it is not to become, like so much of the death of God theology, a victim of a radical process of adaptation.

To amplify this assertion, I should add that theologians must, if communication is to be fruitful, reflect above all about man's unconscious, with which the traditional Christian anthropology was never actively concerned. Since Freud, M. Scheler and H. Plessner have taken this aspect of man into account in philosophy and the members of the Frankfurt school have considered it in their philosophical, sociological and psychoanalytical study of the totality of man. Finally, Lévi-Strauss, the father of structuralism, has insisted that his structural analysis begins, like psychoanalysis, with the unconscious structures[11] underlying such diverse phenomena as morals, cultures and linguistic systems. It is this extension of the analysis of individuals at the unconscious level that gives ethnological and linguistic structuralism its scientific importance.[12] If Christian anthropology is not to remain completely isolated from the psychological study of man by simply making use of certain psychotherapeutic methods from time to time,[13] it must fully assimilate the findings outlined here. It is above all in this sphere that the struggle between those who defend subjectivity and personality and those who uphold the unconscious, anonymous structures will be decided and that Christian humanism will show its true colours, by discussing the present situation in the light of its formal object.

Let me sum up my conclusions by pointing to some of the ways in which Christian anthropology may be able to communicate effectively with the psychological view of man. Firstly, the psychological discovery of the conscious and the unconscious, of the ego and the id and of guided and unguided impulses can be related, for example, to the theological justification of freedom, truthfulness and openness to the world. Secondly, the psychological view of sexuality can be linked with the theological concept of eros and agape and with the Church's norms concerning sexual life. Thirdly, the psychological understanding of infan-

[11] G. Schiwy, *Neue Aspekte des Strukturalismus* (Munich, 1971), pp. 144–148.
[12] *Ibid.*, p. 149.
[13] As, for example, in the preoccupation of certain American theologians with the non-directive method of C. R. Rogers applied to personality change.

tilism and maturity as an individual process can be compared with the theological idea of "coming of age". This list could, of course, be lengthened, but what is more important is to bear in mind that no solution will be found to the problem of communication between Christian anthropology and the psychological understanding of man without taking into account both the biological and the sociological dimensions.

(c) *Theology and Sociology*

The current preoccupation of theologians with sociology is well known. This interest began with the opening of dialogue between Christians and thinkers influenced in different ways by Marxism, for instance, those whose ideas stemmed from Max Weber or Ernst Troeltsch. Many theologians tried to escape from the effects of ideological alienation by following purely positive analyses of modern industrial society which are completely free of ideology.[14] These are valuable in their objective assessment of anthropological facts, such as the rapid development of secondary and tertiary structures, social mobility, the speed of technological advances and their ambivalence as a positive challenge and as a potential alienation, man's anonymity in the metropolis, movements such as women's liberation, and so on. Many theologians, however, recognize that faith implies not only a factual knowledge of the world, but also a will to change it, and regard the political task confronting Christian anthropology as essential. J. Moltmann and J. B. Metz, for example, have indicated the direction which should be followed after lengthy debates with neo-Marxists such as G. Lukács, E. Bloch and others, and have stressed the principles of publicity, praxis and openness to the future and the revolutionary potential of Christianity. This movement has given Christian anthropology the character of a science inspired by Messianism and has thereby enabled it to embrace all the demands made by the dialectics of the Cross and by modern man's struggle for life.

Serious attempts have, for example, been made to bring Christians and neo-Marxists together in dialogue on the subject of

[14] See, for example, A. Gehlen and H. Schelsky, *Soziologie* (Düsseldorf, 1966).

grace,[5] on the basis of the historical resemblance between Jewish-Christian Messianism and the Marxist dialectics of the future,[16] similar aims, the methodical unity of faith and science leading to a unity of theory and praxis, a mutual appreciation of subjectivity and a shared attitude of social criticism. The point of departure for this dialogue is to be found in the dialectics of alienation and liberation, which Paul Tillich had already placed in the centre of his doctrine of redemption.[17] The concept of alienation (estrangement in Tillich) is valuable because it is part of the essential vocabularies of psychology, social philosophy and philosophical anthropology and can be used to describe such traditional theological terms as original sin, the sin of the world, and so on. The contrasting concept, liberation, runs throughout the whole of Paul's teaching about grace and sometimes even has similar social and personal accents to those given to the concept by the neo-Marxists. Communication between Christians and neo-Marxists can therefore open in the concrete with debate firstly about grace and knowledge (science and wisdom), secondly about grace and work (charism and the community-forming function of work together) and thirdly about grace and intersubjective relationships (charis as eros and agape; grace, happiness and sexuality). The following "dynamic" definition of grace should be observed in this context. Grace is a relationship between God and man in which God communicates himself freely to man who becomes himself in history in faith in Christ. Speaking about grace has once more been made not only possible but also meaningful and even profitable by the rediscovery by neo-Marxists of such basic anthropological concepts as subjectivity, love and the conquest of death.[18]

(d) Theology and Philosophy

Since the establishment of dialogue between Christian anthropology on the one hand and biology, psychology and sociology

[15] See my lecture given in the summer of 1972 to the theological faculty of the University of Würzburg.

[16] See R. Garaudy, J. B. Metz and K. Rahner, Der Dialog (Hamburg, 1966), p. 107.

[17] T. Wernsdörfer, Die entfremdete Welt. Eine Untersuchung zur Theologie Paul Tillichs (Zürich, 1968).

[18] See V. Gardavsky, Gott ist nicht ganz tot (Munich, 5th edn., 1971).

on the other, certain philosophies, such as the metaphysics of substance with its inherent dualism, have become closed to communication with Christian anthropology, whereas others, such as existentialism, which Paul Tillich regarded as the natural confederate of Christianity,[19] have reached a crisis. In the recent past, the existentialist concentration on the subject and its insistence on the I-thou relationship have come to be seen as inadequate to represent certain important aspects of contemporary existence. What is more, collective processes have remained almost unknown both in existentialism and in the exact science and have been more easily assimilated by the humane studies. Neo-positivism in general and the philosophy of Wittgenstein in particular, on the other hand, have been widely acclaimed as capable of doing justice to the demands of the natural sciences and of modern technology, but their inadequacy with regard to humanity has been acknowledged.

A new "universal science", which opens a possible perspective on to communication with Christian anthropology, has, however, been introduced by Lévi-Strauss, who has developed his structural analysis within the context of ethnology and sociology and has made use of the method of exact science. Form is regarded as more important than content in structuralism, which is a "method of investigating man as a whole, both in his cosmological and in his historical setting, an aim shared by Scheler and Plessner. In structural analysis, however, this method is so generalized that it can be systematically applied both to individual natural and humane sciences and to philosophical anthropology.[20]

It is above all, however, because of its affinity with linguistic analysis and its consequent aim to interpret totality that structuralism is so relevant to the Christian understanding of man, which it can help to free from its misuse of mystical and of speculative theology, from its ambiguous and excessive employment of the concept of "love" and from its *a priori* tendency either to transcendentalize human existence or to isolate human freedom. It may perhaps also help Christian anthropology to communicate widely with the contemporary biological, psychological, sociological and philosophical views of man and thereby provide

[19] *Systematic Theology*, II (Chicago, 1957; London, 1958).
[20] G. Schiwy, *op. cit.*, p. 148.

an interpretation of totality with a specifically Christian formal principle. This might in turn enable Christians to come to a better understanding of the real questions concerning man's existence and thus better to apply the answers given by Christian revelation to these questions.[21]

We should, however, be alert to the anti-humanistic danger inherent in the structuralists' method and ideology. It is, of course, possible to think in an anti-humanistic way out of respect for the really humane element—this emerged clearly in the debate between J.-P. Sartre and the structuralists,[22] but Christians, in their objectivity, must always continue to defend subjectivity in accordance with the specifically Christian formal object. In this task, Christian anthropology has to proceed critically firstly, whenever an excessive determinism of unconscious structures threatens to destroy man's freedom of choice (his faith!); secondly, if the possibility of a uniquely subjective meaning is denied to the objective structures of speech; thirdly, when praxis, as the factor which changes the world, is defined as "imprisoned in the ultimately unchangeable structure";[23] and fourthly, if historicity and hope in the future are presented as illusory. In all this, if it is to be capable of communication, the new Christian anthropology must remain fully conscious of its specifically Christian identity and continue to present the constantly "new" eschatological dimension of man's existence.

Translated by David Smith

[21] See G. Schiwy's stimulating discussions, *op. cit.*, pp. 168–83.
[22] J. Lacroix, *Le sens de l'athéisme moderne* (Tournai, 6th edn., 1970), pp. 74–104.
[23] G. Schiwy, *op. cit.*, p. 186.

Wolfhart Pannenberg

The Christological Foundation
of Christian Anthropology

I

DOES anthropology need a christological foundation? At first sight, the opposite would seem to be the case, since christology has always been influenced by man's changing understanding of himself. The fact that christology has been historically conditioned by the soteriological interest is so important that christological ideas can even be regarded as projections of the principal interpretations of human existence. During the Hellenistic period, for instance, man sought deification in overcoming transience, whereas medieval man looked for reconciliation with God in overcoming guilt. Luther modified this medieval quest by trusting in God in the experience of judgment. During the Enlightenment, morality was regarded as the basis of the human community, in the romantic period the unity of the personality was sought and, in the modern age, we are above all concerned with man's person as opposed to the objective world of technology and the changes that it causes in human relationships.

What is meant by saying that all these anthropological ideas have been expressed in christological terms? Since Christians have always seen true humanity and made possible to all mankind in the figure of Jesus Christ, Jesus has been represented as the Messiah, as God-man, as the reconciler, as the one whose sufferings are representative, as the one who is perfect and blessed because of his consciousness of God, as the one who lives entirely from the divine Thou and is therefore over and against and independent of the world.

If these were simply reflections in the figure of Jesus of various anthropological views, then christology would be no more than an ideal interpretation of perfect humanity. But this is not so—the view of man they express is guaranteed not by human existence, but only by the history of that one man. This is a very great claim and we are bound to ask whether the general anthropological views which are simply given a concrete and ideal form in the figure of Jesus are not opposed to it. Ought we not to be able to prove that a change takes place in those general anthropological views in the light of the history of the one man Jesus of Nazareth?

It is in fact not only possible to verify this, but also to decide in this way whether, in christological ideas as opposed to their real intention, it is only a question of secondary reflections in the figure of Jesus of anthropological views with a different basis or whether christology itself ought to have a constitutive value for general anthropology. This second possibility is not invalidated by christology referring to the anthropological views given to it from other sources. This ought only to be avoided if the relationship between christology and history were decontinuous, in which case the incarnation could not have been an historical event. A discontinuous event of revelation could not provide a positive answer to the question concerning man's essential nature, the question that man has asked throughout his history and not simply since the coming of Jesus Christ. But the history of Jesus Christ does contribute constitutively towards the answer to this anthropological question, not by providing an entirely new point of departure, but by including within itself and thus transforming the already existing reality of man and his historical question about himself.

II

The reality of man as created and fashioned at the beginning of time is interpreted mythologically in the Bible. Adam is not merely the first man—he is man as such, whose history is repeated in all individual men and provides the key to what conditions their existence. The Greek philosophers from Parmenides to Plato were no longer dependent on this mythological tradition going back to the beginning of time; they were concerned with the everlasting, unchanging reality underlying the changing phenomena of the world. This was also the *ousia* or essential being of man.

A radical change in man's understanding of himself was introduced by the coming of Christ—the first Adam was confronted by a new, second Adam, who was not simply a "living being", but also a "life-giving spirit" (1 Cor. 15. 45 ff.). The first, original man was no longer the highest and the second man was no longer, as in Philo's contrast between the two accounts of creation (Gen. 1 and 2),[1] a purely earthly man placed behind the first, heavenly man. The second Adam far surpassed the first. Paul completely reverses Philo's order of the first and second men in the two creation stories and applies them to Christ so as to illustrate the far-reaching implications of his appearance for man. For Paul, the first man was earthly and mortal and the second was heavenly and immortal. Only Christ, the second man, was in the likeness of God (2 Cor. 4. 4) and it was only when men were united with Christ in baptism that they could share in this likeness of God (Rom. 8. 29; cf. Col. 3. 10). At the same time, however, Paul also includes in his teaching the traditional view (Gen. 1. 26) that man—rather than woman—is distinguished by the fact that he is made in the likeness of God (1 Cor. 11. 7). The early Christian fathers overcame the tension between these two views by teaching that Christ was the primordial image, whereas the first man was created in the likeness of, that is as a copy of, God. The union with the new man who appeared in Christ became evident when the visible appearance of the primordial image in the incarnation perfected the copy of God in us.[2]

It is only in the light of such an interpretation that the essential concept of man was, by the single saving event in history, made fluid and became what Ignatius of Antioch called (*Ad Eph.* 20. 1) a saving economy leading to the new man. Even in the teaching of Irenaeus, the idea that the first man was created in the likeness of God and that this likeness was perfected by Jesus Christ is seen as a bracket enclosing the beginning and the end of this road to unity in the history of man and thus avoiding the danger

---

[1] Philo, *Leg. All.*, I, 31; *Opif Mundi*, 134 ff.
[2] Irenaeus, *Adv. Haer.* V, 16 1 f.

of a gnostic dualism between the first, earthly man and the second, heavenly man.[3]

Whereas man's essential nature is regarded in philosophy as invariable, in Christian teaching it is seen as a history from the first to the second man and as completed by its supernatural destiny. This teaching is close to the concept of a naturally conditioned human existence as man's original state in the history in which his being is resolved. This original state is characterized by openness towards his supernatural fulfilment, which is already present as a future destiny and thus corresponds to the single saving event in history.

This fact has again and again been misrepresented in Christian anthropology by the use of Gen. 2 to show man's original state as one of paradisiacal perfection and his redemption as a restoration to that state. This view does not, however, do full justice to the Christian conviction of the definitive importance of the salvation that appeared in Jesus Christ. According to Paul, the first man was not in a state of perfection and Irenaeus represented the primordial state as a weak copy of the likeness of God that first appeared in Christ, claiming that he could understand the possibility of sin because of man's original state of weakness (*Adv. Haer.* IV, 38; cf. III, 23, 5). On the other hand, the task of exonerating the creator from the sins of his creatures—the theodicy —is made easier if this state is regarded as perfect, although it becomes almost impossible to incorporate a Christian understanding of man into a purely natural anthropology if this teaching about man's original state of perfection is maintained.

As early as the eighteenth century, this teaching was abandoned by J. G. Herder, who saw man's original state as openness to the unfulfilled destiny of becoming the likeness of God, and thus laid the foundations for M. Scheler's modern anthropology of openness to the world. "You gave instinct to the animals," Herder wrote, "and engraved your image, religion and humanity in the heart of man. The outline of the columns can be seen there in deep, dark marble, but he cannot carve and fashion them himself. Only tradition, teaching, reason and experience can do that

[3] H. Langerbeck, *Aufsätze zur Gnosis*, ed. H. Dörries (Göttingen, 1967), p. 56.

and you have not left him without means.'"[4] Herder does not
use the term "second Adam", but speaks of "religion and
humanity" and, whereas Irenaeus referred to the Spirit and the
prophets, he speaks of "tradition, teaching, reason and experience". Unlike the twentieth-century social psychologist A.
Gehlen, however, Herder knew that man cannot "carve" himself
into the likeness, the outline of which is present in his heart.
He did not see man as the "active being" who transforms what
is lacking in his original state by activity into advantages and
thus creates himself.[5]

III

Christology can contribute positively to our understanding of
man if his original state is seen as being one of openness to his
future destiny and if he himself is regarded as possessing a
fundamentally new aim, that of moving in history towards the
salvation that has appeared in Christ. For Paul, this fundamentally new element was given in the second Adam and consisted
of the life that appeared in Christ's resurrection. The early fathers
were also completely in the Pauline tradition in going against the
Greek claim that the soul was in itself immortal[6] and insisting
that the immortality mediated by the second Adam applied not
only to the soul but also to the body, so that the whole man had
to be seen as history moving towards the life that has appeared in
Christ.

Modern man tends to reject the traditional Christian hope of
life beyond death as a flight from the present reality and to look
in life here and now for the meaning of Jesus, concentrating
especially on the love and human fellowship that he represented

---

[4] J. G. Herder, *Ideen zur Philosophie der Geschichte der Menschheit*
(1784), IX, 5; see also, for the meaning of this idea in Herder, H. Sunnus,
Die Wurzeln des modernen Menschenbildes bei J. G. Herder (Nürnberg,
1971), especially pp. 32 ff.

[5] A. Gehlen, *Der Mensch, seine Natur und seine Stellung in der Welt*
(Bonn, 6th edn., 1958). Gehlen, however, is convinced that he is completely in the tradition of Herder; see pp. 88 ff.

[6] See Irenaeus, *Adv. Haer.* II, 34, 4; see also, III, 19, 1; V, 21, 3. See also
H. A. Wolfson, "Immortality and Resurrection in the Philosophy of the
Church Fathers", in K. Stendahl, ed., *Immortality and Resurrection* (New
York, 1965), pp. 54 ff., especially pp. 56 ff.

in his own life. Although there can be no doubt of the central importance of love in Jesus' message, the meaning that Jesus gives to love is not self-evident. It cannot be understood without ambiguity either in his turning towards the lost or in his insistence that one's enemies should not be resisted, because he himself was in constant conflict with his opponents.

Clearly, Jesus' idea of love has to be understood in close conjunction with his eschatological proclamation of the Kingdom of God, in which he perceived evidence of God's love. The salvation of the lost, as reported, for example, in the three parables of Luke 15. 4–32, takes place through Jesus, because the one who accepts Jesus and his message of the nearness of the Kingdom is no longer separated from God. His sins are forgiven and the Kingdom is already present for him, even though it still lies in the future. This presence of the future Kingdom in man's acceptance of Jesus' message is the act of God's saving love, precisely because it is linked to the forgiveness of sins. The love of one's neighbour taught by Jesus is rooted in this forgiving love of God, who turns towards those who are lost. (See, for instance, the parables of the unforgiving debtor, Matt. 18. 23–35, and of the prodigal son, Luke 15. 11–32, and the fifth petition of the Our Father, Matt. 6. 12, all of which illustrate in different ways the giving and receiving of forgiveness as an essential aspect of God's universal love.)

Jesus' concern for human fellowship can therefore be understood unambiguously in the light of his eschatological message as a sharing in God's forgiving love made visible in Jesus himself and thus as communion with God himself. Even before Jesus, the Jewish rabbis stressed the primacy of love and the idea of human fellowship was certainly not unknown outside Judaism. Jesus, however, above all emphasized that the Kingdom of God is in the man who accepted his message and it is this emphasis that makes the idea of love and human fellowship so characteristic of his teaching.

If, however, we do not regard this love simply and solely as human fellowship, but as a sharing in God's love for the world and thus as a sharing in the reality of God himself, we will be less remote from the Pauline definition of salvation as eternal life which has appeared in the resurrection of Jesus than we seem to be at first sight. The enduring quality of this new life is to be found in its connection with the divine origin of all life, in other words, with the Spirit of God, which is for Paul the Spirit of the love of God, which appeared in Jesus Christ and especially in his death for sinners (Rom. 5. 8). Nothing can "separate us from the love of God in Jesus Christ" (Rom. 8. 39) and for this reason Paul's hope is directed towards a sharing in life which is closely connected with the Spirit of God and which has appeared in his resurrection to Jesus. The Spirit, love and life therefore are most closely united and, in Paul's teaching, Christian love can be understood as a dwelling of the Spirit of God in the heart of the believer, arousing him to eternal life. What, however, will be made manifest in the future in Christians as the new life of the resurrection is already present in them through the Spirit. In this way, Paul brings out the emphasis that Jesus himself placed on the presence of the future Kingdom.

John stressed the connection between the love of God and his presence even more than Paul, insisting that this love had appeared with Jesus (John 3. 16) and that it was a bond between the Father, the Son and the believer (John 15. 9 ff.; 17. 26; 1 John 4. 7 ff.), since "God is love, and he who abides in love abides in God, and God abides in him" (1 John 4. 16). It is clear too that John does not regard the love of God as identical with human fellowship, which, he believes, is derived from and derives its meaning and orientation from the love of God: "We love, because he first loved us" (1 John 4. 19; cf. 4. 10). Christian love is primarily not a question of a human relationship, but of the presence of God's love in the world and man's sharing in this.

In Christian ethics, love is the most important element of all, not founded in subjective feelings or measured according to the wishes of the one to whom it is directed, but, on the contrary, always alert to what the recipient needs in God's eyes. It recognizes that recipient as God's creature, who can perceive God's love for the world and share in it.

We may conclude this section by saying that the salvation that appeared in Jesus Christ consists of man's sharing in God's life, both his hope of eternal life and Christian love being involved in this. Whereas this hope is directed towards the future Kingdom of God which has already appeared to Jesus in his resurrection, Christian love is concerned with the presence of God, towards whose future the hope of resurrection is directed. Paul was therefore able to speak in this light of Christ as the second Adam, not only with reference to the new life which appeared with Jesus (1 Cor. 15. 45), but also with regard to Christ's obedience to the will of God (Rom. 5. 12 ff.). In both cases, the same reality is involved—that of the new man, united with God.

IV

The new man of God who appeared in Jesus Christ did not replace the old man in that the first man disappeared. All men are still born as the first man, as a "living being" rather than as a "life-giving spirit", but the new man grows in them by faith and baptism and by the working of the Spirit and the love of God. What does this reality of the new man mean for the first man?

In the first place, the first man is only man in so far as he is related to the man who is united with God, the man who he is destined to become. This is a fact which is not taken sufficiently into account by modern biological, psychological and sociological anthropology. If Christian anthropology were to adapt itself to this situation as though it were simply a question of an attitude towards research into the study of man, it would sacrifice its specifically Christian character. Christians are, however, bound to ask why man's being constituted in relation to God and why he is characterized by being religious are so neglected by modern non-Christian anthropology. They are, however, also bound to recognize that even this form of anthropology still deals *de facto* with man whose being is constituted in relation to God. The man who turns away from God does not, after all, cease to be man whose destiny is unity with God.

In the second place, man is not only *de facto* not yet the same as the new man who is united with God—he also does not see himself as having this destiny. He sees himself as already possessing the fullness of humanity, even as he is now and even if he is conscious of being alienated from his humanity, because, when he is conscious of this alienation and resolved to overcome it, he is certainly in possession of his humanity.

It has to be borne in mind that the word "man" is used here in the sense of man as history moving towards a still unfulfilled destiny. Modern man is still living in the transitional phase and it is not yet clear what he will become. His consciousness of alienation and his concern to overcome it imply a claim that he knows his destiny. Ought this knowledge not to be regarded as adequate, so that man's alienation can be seen to exist and his concern to overcome it lead him to his goal? In that case, is the man with this adequate knowledge not already at the goal, even though this known goal is not yet realized? On the other hand, how can man have this adequate knowledge about what is not yet clear? It is only possible if the process which connects his present with his future destiny is one of self-realization.

This brings us to the heart of the problem, which can be defined as our understanding of freedom. Self-realization presupposes a freedom that is conscious of itself. It is true that freedom can only be gained in the process of self-realization, but freedom is also presupposed so that it can be gained by self-realization, which is therefore a process of realizing this freedom by overcoming the obstacles in its way. Man has, after all, to overcome everything that prevents him from freely developing. This presupposes that he is in himself already free and in possession of his identity. It does not take into account the fact that he may be remote from his identity, a sinner.

In Christian anthropology, since the first man is not free, he cannot be identified with his destiny,[7] and therefore needs to be set free in order to become himself: "if the Son makes you free, you will be free indeed" (John 8. 36), cf. "where the Spirit of the Lord is, there is freedom" (2 Cor. 3. 17). This is a direct consequence of the fundamental assumption that the first man is not yet in possession of his destiny—he only possesses it with the appearance of Jesus Christ.

In the history of theology, this concept of freedom has become obscured because of the application of the idea of freedom of choice, which was first used in the debate with the gnostics in order to show that evil did not originate with the creator, but with Lucifer and the first man. This freedom of choice, how-

[7] In this case, I am thinking of freedom as identity with being oneself; for "freedom of choice", see below.

ever, is not unconnected with freedom in the first sense, that of self-identity, because choice presupposes identity with the subject who chooses and at least an implicit consciousness of that identity. It is not necessarily a question of true identity or of true human freedom, however. Even when a man lacks freedom on the basis of false identity, he still has freedom of choice. On the other hand, the range of possibilities of choice on the basis of identity achieved needs to be no greater than it is where there is a lack of existential freedom. It is in fact smaller, because the identity of the subject itself anticipates certain possibilities of choice so that, if that identity is not questioned, the range of possibilities from which a choice can be made is limited by that identity and not by external circumstances.

In the West, then, too little attention has been given by theologians to man's identity as presupposing a range of possible choices, with the result that there has been a long and futile controversy about grace and freedom of choice. As a consequence of this, theology has played an essential part in the development of the modern view of man as a free subject. Now, however, this view is seriously questioned—can the identity of the subject be thought of as already given in advance to conscious life or is it not better to say that it is constituted, changed and reconstituted in a life history?

Fichte's original insight was that it was not possible for the subject to establish and to guarantee the unity of itself. The problem had arisen because of Kant's teaching that the unity of the self-consciousness ought to establish the unity of experience, but that self-consciousness becomes the self that knows itself. Fichte tried to find the unity of these two elements by accepting a self-projection of the ego, but was obliged to admit that it was not possible to regard self-consciousness as the result of a self-projection.[8] The consciousness can only accept the unity of itself, its identity and therefore also its freedom as given. What has to be distinguished in this unity is how it represents itself to the consciousness. It is, however, not possible to regard such a concretization of the identity for the consciousness as a projection of the consciousness because the consciousness is only given as a unity

[8] See D. Heinrich, *Fichtes ursprüngliche Einsicht* (Frankfurt, 1967).

in such a concretization and does not precede it as a unity of the subject.

There is, then, clearly a connection between Fichte's problem and the modern psychological problem of identity. It is therefore all the more remarkable that, since Freud, psychologists have defined the stages in identification as self-identification, as though it were possible to presuppose a subject in this process, even though it would be through that process that the identity of the ego would be formed. The social psychologist G. H. Mead avoids this inconsistency by recognizing the self as constituted by society and by regarding the ego as the individual's answer to that self.[9] But can the ego be separated from the self in this way? What still remains to be explained is above all how the "individual" can reply to this identification through society without being an ego which is identical with itself.

Although it is less and less widely accepted nowadays that the identity of the subject and also of the subject's freedom with regard to the process of its experience is already given, such ideas as self-determination, self-realization, self-development and emancipation are still current. Since they include the identity of the subject as a presupposition, however, they too have become unacceptable.

In recent decades, the idea of a transcendental freedom of the subject which precedes all concrete experience has completely changed the Christian understanding of freedom, so that we now see man as not free in himself, but as having to be set free in order to achieve true freedom, a true identity of himself with his destiny. What is more, even this destiny is not in himself already—it can only be found beyond him in God and in the new Adam, the man who is united with God. It is possible that the Christian viewpoint will find a more favourable hearing if Christians no longer insist on the identity of the subject and of the freedom of the subject as something previously given, especially because the idea of freedom as given in history is not in any way opposed to subjectivity. On the contrary, it provides the possibility of a definitive foundation for human subjectivity and freedom, which is not already present before history. It is rather

[9] G. H. Mead, *Mind, Self and Society* (1934) (Chicago, 1965), pp. 135 ff.

the very theme of the history of the individual and of society. The consequence of this history is that man is set free to the freedom of the Spirit possessed by the Son as the man who is united with God. It is only in this light that man can recognise his past history as the history of a search for himself, resulting in failure, sin and alienation from God and from himself.

V

This problem of freedom is a good example of the effects of the christological view of human nature as an historical process which has resulted from the appearance of the new man. The same problem can also be seen in a different form in the Greek idea of reason. Man was regarded by the Greeks as the being who shared in the *logos*, the divine plan of being, and this was expressed in thought and speech, both of which were described in Greek as *logos*. Firstly, in Christian teaching, the divine Logos appeared fully for the first time in history in Jesus Christ, who was the first fully rational being and therefore the first full man. Secondly, the unity between the divine Logos and the man Jesus is not simply supernatural—it is also the first rational realization of human nature according to the Greek understanding of man as a rational being, with the result that the distinction between the divine and the human in the incarnate Logos is as difficult to accept as the unity of the two distinct aspects. Thirdly, faith in the incarnation of the Logos in Jesus Christ also implies an historical understanding of reason in man himself—pre-Christian reason is an anticipation of what became an event in Jesus Christ's becoming man. All reason would, in that case, be constituted not only by the idea of God, but also by this anticipation of the unity of the divine and the human in Jesus Christ.

This anticipation would only take place under the restricting conditions of an historical situation in which the fullness of the Logos had not yet appeared. Even in the history of Jesus, however, the future of God is only present in that it is at the same time also future. It is also an anticipation of a special kind, by which the future of God becomes present as love. What does this mean for our understanding of the fullness of the Logos in Christ? What is the relationship between reason and love in this?

To what degree does the merging together of these two elements point beyond a purely rational, intellectual understanding of reason and beyond a specifically Western understanding of man as a purely "rational animal"? Finally, what does this merging together mean for the possibility of freedom in the Pauline and Johannine sense?

Most of these questions have been given very little attention in Christian theology, which has become accustomed to regard man's reason as part of the "natural" man, thus resulting in a loss of interest in the historical character of reason to which faith in the incarnation of the Logos in Jesus Christ should lead and this faith itself coming to be seen as irrational, in other words, as to be accepted only on authority. The increasing anti-thesis between reason and the authority of the Christian tradition inevitably led to an increasing obscurity in Christian teaching with regard to human freedom, with the consequence that freedom came to be seen as rational and as anti-authoritarian.

VI

In Christianity, Jesus, the new man, is not simply opposed to the old man. He is the new man in that he realizes in himself the original destiny of man, that of community with God and in that he was in a special way an ordinary man. This special aspect of his humanity is to be found in his mission to proclaim the Kingdom of God and in his distinction between the future of God and his own present. He staked everything on this future beyond himself and it was precisely because of this that God's future became present in him. This "beyond himself" or "beyond oneself" is what characterizes the Christian understanding of freedom and what is echoed in the fundamental proposition of man's self-transcendence or eccentricity in modern anthropology,[10] although it is not clear in the latter what is the centre that makes

---

[10] H. Plessner's concept of eccentricity comes closest to the formulae of openness to the world and of self-transcendence as a mark of man's special position among living beings; see especially, H. Plessner, *Die Stufen des Organischen und der Mensch* (1928) (Berlin, 2nd edn., 1965), especially pp. 288 ff., 309 ff.; see also, *idem., Conditio humana* (Pfullingen, 1964), pp. 49 ff.

it possible for man to stand outside himself and thus to become capable of rational and generalized reflection. In the case of Jesus, this centre was certainly outside himself—it was the God who was to come, the Father. In distinguishing himself from God and his future, Jesus was following his divine mission and at the same time at one with God. This is the historical origin and the constant norm of what is nowadays called man's personality in the sense of his being a person and in so far as this means that the individual is not a person for himself alone, but as I over and against a Thou. This view of man as a person, according to which the ego or "I" comes not from himself, but from beyond himself, from a Thou, originates, of course, in the personal concept of the Trinity, the Son being Son not from himself, but from his relationship with the Father.[11] The application of this trinitarian idea to anthropology, in which personalism has been known since the time of Feuerbach, can only be regarded as correct in a very limited sense if a Thou in the form of a fellow human instead of the divine Thou constitutes the "I" in his state of being a person, since man cannot receive his destiny unconditionally from a human Thou in the way in which Jesus received his destiny from the future of his Father. It is only where the human Thou is distinguished from God and, by his being there, points to that God who is different from him that God can become present to the I through the human Thou and constitute that I as a person. This is because the love of God comes close to him and sets him free in the form of a fellow man. This was what those who came close to him in faith experienced in Jesus.

Boethius' definition of the person as a rational individual[12] is not necessarily in conflict with the trinitarian view, but Christian anthropology has to work out, in a different way from Boethius, what it means to be a rational individual. The individuality not only of Jesus, but also of every man, is rationally constituted by his distinction from God and by the eccentricity of his trust in God's future, at least in so far as his destiny is a movement to-

---

[11] See my article "Person", *Religion in Geschichte und Gegenwart*, V (1961), pp. 230–5, especially pp. 231 ff.

[12] Boethius, *MPL*, 64, 1343, C (*De Personis et duabus naturis*, 3).

wards a complete likeness of God which appeared in Jesus Christ
in the unity of God and man.

Translated by David Smith

PART II
BULLETIN

Georges Crespy

The Image of Man according to Vatican II and Uppsala 1968

MY AIM in this bulletin is to compare the Constitution *Gaudium et Spes* on the Church in the Modern World and certain documents issued by the World Council of Churches at Uppsala in 1968. In the light of the present crisis in humanism, I shall analyse above all the image of man that emerges from these documents. First of all, however, we must examine the character of the texts themselves.

Firstly, *Gaudium et Spes* is a definitive conciliar text, approved as canonical, written in Latin and officially signed on 7 December 1965. The documents of the World Council of Churches do not set out to achieve this status. They appeared spasmodically and are usually applied to specific circumstances. They were until recently published simultaneously in three languages but this has now been increased to four as a Russian text has been added. We are therefore never concerned with one single text but with four separate texts for, as I think is generally recognized, a translation does in some sense establish a *new text*. For the purpose of this paper, I must therefore choose one of the documents and decide to study it in one of the four languages. For the sake of convenience, I shall take the "Message" of the Uppsala Conference, drawing also on the reports of the various study groups (*Uppsala Speaks*, Geneva, 1968).

Secondly, the Uppsala "Message" and *Gaudium et Spes* came into being in rather different ways. We can actually trace the history of *Gaudium et Spes* in the sense that we can study the various versions it went through before it was finally promulgated. The Uppsala document is quite different—it is simply the record of what was said in the debates at the Assembly and to promulgate and to record are two very distinct things. The person who studies the documents must take this fact carefully into account.

Thirdly, the form and structure of the two documents are quite different. *Gaudium et Spes* consists of carefully presented statements each of which is firmly anchored in a previous supportive section. The document is also carefully related to the preamble (*proemium*). The Uppsala document is based on a series of unrelated questions which the text tries to gather up and edit into a coherent whole. It does not attempt to establish doctrine so much as to present a series of exhortations. According to Jakobsen's terms, *Gaudium et Spes* is designed to have a basically normative function whereas the Uppsala document is designed to provide the incentive for theological endeavour. The reason for this is perfectly simple—the member Churches of the World Council have no single theological frame of reference while the Church of Rome is supposed to, at least in theory. This distinction is absolutely fundamental.

Both documents open with rather abstract statements: "The joys and the hopes, the griefs and the anxieties of the men of this age . . ." (*Gaudium et Spes*, 1) and "the excitement . . . the protest . . . the clash . . ." (Uppsala). Whereas the latter, however, stresses the need for listening ("In this climate the Uppsala Assembly met first of all to listen"), *Gaudium et Spes* does not neglect this element of listening ("this community realizes that it is truly and intimately linked with mankind and its history", 1), but emphasizes how the Church thinks and acts. The message of Uppsala insists on the need to show "something of the newness which Christ will complete", but there is no reference to traditional Christian teaching. In the first case, there is evidence of a tradition which has to be verified; in the second, a praxis is sought. In both cases, the situation has evoked an attempt to renew the language of faith.

What we must now examine are the basic assumptions underlying the two texts. In both cases it is assumed that the documents are based on knowledge which gives the power to scrutinize the "signs of the times" (*signa temporum scrutare*) though what is the source, origin and basis of the knowledge is nowhere stated. To be precise, *Gaudium et Spes* creates a kind of dialectical tension between theology and anthropology while the "Message" of Uppsala is based much more upon an assessment of the contemporary situation, a situation to which it endeavours to preach the gospel. More than this, however, *Gaudium et Spes* works on the assumption that there is such a thing as salvation-history and that from this assumption certain assertions should be made. The world, which Christians believe to be founded on (*conditum*) and preserved (*conservatum*) by the love of God, has fallen under the power of sin. Through the death and resurrection of Jesus Christ the power of Satan has been shattered. The world has thus been redeemed in order to be transformed (*secundum propositum Dei transformetur*) and this in order that it should reach its true consummation (*consummatio*). The rapid and often violent changes which take place in the world (*mutatio*) can be seen to obscure the eternal and perennial values (*valores perennes*) which must be continually reaffirmed. How then does this *transformatio* of God operate in the *mutatio* of the world?

First of all, what is the exact nature of the *mutatio* of which we are speaking? It can be seen, for example, in the growth of forces of which man is less and less the master. Examples of this change are an increase in freedom accompanied by an increase in enslavement by the forces of society, a search for unity accompanied by pluralism and discord, a growth in intellectual communication accompanied by the increasing diversity of "language", an increasing organization accompanied by growing spiritual stagnation and an increasing ability to manage and organize time accompanied by a deepening sense of the uncontrollable speed of change. The inevitable conclusion is that we are dealing with a process which is fundamentally dialectic.

Now, if we turn to the message of Uppsala, we are immediately faced with a theological infrastructure of a very different kind. The document begins with the discoveries of science and technology and their implications (technology is only mentioned once in *Gaudium et Spes*, 5), and on this basis it tries to point to the true sources of hope for the human race. This is also accompanied by specific judgments about the aberrations of the human race. For example, it points out that men have increasingly become each other's neighbours, though this has not been accompanied by any growth in the understanding of how to live together and this is just as true of Christians as of anyone else. It also points to the chasm between rich and poor and to the fact that the Churches have hardly even begun to glimpse at the true meaning of universal community. The document does not attempt to talk anthropologically—it is more concerned to make certain specific assertions grounded in faith alone. "God makes all things new." But does this really give enough emphasis to the *transformatio* as opposed to the *mutatio*?

It is true that at this point the two documents have certain similarities. They both presuppose a tension between the transforming activity of God and the movements for change which characterize the endeavours of the human race at the present time. But the questions that both documents pose is whether there is ever a close relationship between the *transformatio* and the *mutatio*, whether the two actually ever coincide, and whether it is possible that they should do so while allowing each to have its own function.

In order to preserve this tension, the Church must continually look for new forms for the content of its message. It must address itself to areas of meaning in which its message stands in opposition and even offers a kind of counter-meaning which it alone can give. The importance of this is far more obvious in *Gaudium et Spes* than it is in the Uppsala document. *Gaudium et Spes* begins with a point of reference from which it draws various threads. It weaves these threads in turn into the fabric of a theological anthropology. Uppsala tries to draw together the various contributions and then attempts to preach a message on that basis. As we have seen, this most often takes the form of specific assertions. In studying the Uppsala document, we can see what was actually discarded in the process of working towards the final document itself. With *Gaudium et Spes*, by parallel, we can watch the process whereby all the material was carefully integrated and assimilated into the central corpus of the document itself. The conciliar anthropology was closed at first, but opened up step by step, while that of Uppsala which was so open at the outset coagulated step by step. Even in spite of this it never arrived at the stage where it could provide a schema which would act as a guide to the Church in its pastoral mission.

Is this difference we have been describing self-evident in the content of the documents themselves? To answer this, we must try to see what view of man both texts hold out to the world, and see in what respects they differ. A striking difference is revealed at the very beginning—Uppsala refers again and again to recent events such as "the protest of student revolts, the shock of assassinations, the clash of wars". If one adds to this "the excitement of new scientific discoveries" (though these are never specified), one has a strong impression of the facts which "mark the year 1968" and which conditioned the "climate" in which the Assembly was held. The point of departure, then, is the world here and now, with the "cry of those who long for peace; of the hungry and exploited who demand bread and justice; of the victims of discrimination . . . and of the increasing millions who seek for the meaning of life". Precisely who these people are is, however, not stated. The man to whom we listen ("we heard the cry of those . . .") is the man whom we see present in the world today in the situations listed in the message.

On the other hand, *Gaudium et Spes* starts with man's existential situation (*pauperum presertim et quorumvis affectum*). Note the title *Gaudium et Spes* (as opposed to *Luctus et Angor*)—the contrast is not peculiar to 1965 alone. Moreover, the generic terms "mankind", "human family", and so on, are used instead of "men", thus emphasizing historical continuity.

One could express the difference between the two documents in this way. In the first case, history is taken into account within the context of a specific historical situation. In the second case, history is seen as a process which in itself contains meaning of crucial importance. If this appraisal is fair, then the existential presuppositions of *Gaudium et Spes* are somewhat deceptive. In a sense the Uppsala document is the more existential of the two. Take, for example, Section II of the report which talks about the "nature" of man ("men can know their true nature only if they see themselves as sons of God" is a statement which assumes the relational importance of human nature). This nature is already transformed by the coming of the "new man Jesus Christ", the "head of the new humanity". This new humanity is not an end

in itself—it is a gift. The Uppsala document demonstrates this
by three false syllogisms. The major premise is that man is lost,
the minor is that Christ is the new man and the conclusion is
that we must give our consent to this new humanity in Christ.
There is a growing gulf between rich and poor. Christians who
deny the dignity of man deny the dignity of Christ. The consequence is that we must fight for a human community, the principle of which is justice.

But who or what has made man what he is now? In *Gaudium
et Spes* 6 and 7, there is a series of statements made in the
present tense. "The industrial type of society is gradually being
spread . . ."; "new . . . media of social communication . . . are
giving the swiftest and widest possible circulation to styles of
thought and feeling"; "Man's ties with his fellows are constantly
being multiplied"; "this kind of evolution can be seen . . ."; "a
change in attitudes . . . calls accepted values into question"; "the
institutions, laws . . . as handed down . . . do not always seem to
be well adapted . . ."; "these new conditions have their impact
on religion." These statements are, of course, imprecise and generalized. They call for further economic and social application
but they are principles on which it would be hard to disagree.
They do not have strong ideological content, which would immediately arouse controversy and disagreement. So, for example
again, the discussion is of industrial society and not of capitalism
or communism, of communication and not of propaganda, of increasingly complex human relationships and not of class conflict.
In this way, it can be seen that the contribution of the humane
sciences, of Marxism, of psychoanalysis to our understanding of
the modern world is only taken into account implicitly. In fact
it is included in a hermeneutical understanding which is based
on the assumption that man is the object and not the subject of
historical process. Modernity as a criterion is considered untrust-
worthy, since it excludes the possibility of a God who is active in
history. Such an approach makes man responsible for the course
of history. One could argue that there are suggestions of this in
the document itself. In the sections on atheism (20 and 21), the
view that man is "an end unto himself" seems to be implied, but
this is at once repudiated and the authors affirm that "every man

remains to himself an unsolved puzzle" and that "only God fully and most certainly provides an answer".

One could also level criticism of this kind at the Uppsala document. "Science today furnishes us with constantly increasing knowledge about man's inner being and his interdependence with society" (Section II, 1.7), but it does not elaborate this. Certainly there is no atheistic emphasis and atheism as a whole is only referred to in passing in the paragraph concerned with dialogue with "men of other faiths or of no faith" (II, 1.6). This is taken up again in the general discussion on secularization (Section IV).

By using such phrases as "our common humanity", "our common concern for that humanity" and "our sharing in new forms of community and common service", basic questions are raised for Christians about their true identity. This is not just a concession to modernity, but a recognition of the importance of relating the contemporary situation to the insights of faith. This in turn leads to a condemnation of those who refuse to identify themselves as sons of God: "The final goal of history was assured, when Christ as head of that new humanity will sum up all things" (Section II. 1.3).

Here once again we come to the theme of *transformatio*. It is clearly conceived of differently in the two texts but this is because there is some divergence about the basic nature of *mutatio*.

For *Gaudium et Spes, mutatio* has purpose and meaning only in relation to a perennial image of man. This implies a kind of theological anthropology where the various elements are woven together but where man is still the agent. The message of Uppsala never discusses the doctrine of man in relation to the doctrine of creation. *Mutatio* is considered purely and simply in the light of christology, a christology which is approached anthropologically (Jesus as the "new man"). It thus remains open and is not confined by any dogmatic definition.

It can therefore be seen that the impact of contemporary humanism has provided *Gaudium et Spes* with a "feed-back" for its attempt to redefine the Church's teaching and has at the same time allowed it to remain open without in any way diminishing its doctrinal content. The feed-back of modern humanism on the Uppsala document is, in a sense, much less, with the result that the reader is conscious of an often disordered and even hesitant attempt to mark out new positions occupied by God in the new positions occupied by man.

In conclusion, we may say that this can best be understood by returning to my remarks about the character and the evolution of the two documents at the beginning of this bulletin. To these remarks, I may add that the aim of one document was to explain, whereas that of the other was to exhort, with the result that their structure and mode of expression are very different. It is therefore interesting to observe that the declarations of the Church's teaching office have to some extent confirmed the teaching of *Gaudium et Spes*, whereas the work of the commission on "Humanum Studies" and especially that of its director, David E. Jenkins, have given rise to even more questions. On the other hand, since these questions are addressed not only to the Councils of the past, but also to the changes that are taking place in the life of mankind today, it is probable that they will prepare the way for a common ground for anthropological discussion.

Translated by Robin Baird-Smith

Jean-Yves Jolif

Marxism and Humanism

"THE source of both the strength and the weakness of Marxism was that it was the most radical attempt to explain the historical process as a whole. For twenty years now, however, its shadow has darkened history; Marxism has stopped living with history, and, through its bureaucratic conservatism, is trying to reduce change to identity." This was Sartre's proclamation, in *Question de méthode* (1960), of the paralysis of Marxism. A few years earlier, in 1957, the Jesuits Bigo, Chambre and Calvez, who had written important works on Marx and the Soviet Union, had refused to take part in a public debate with communists on these subjects. Such a debate, they explained, would be pointless "until the French communists have published serious scientific studies of the Soviet Union and its founder, Karl Marx. This is not at present the case."[1]

We are not going to ask if these judgments were justified. The communists themselves admit that the last ten years have been for them a period of "theoretical reactivation", and that they have had to ask many questions about Marxist philosophy and begin a revaluation of the classical heritage.[2] What is more, if we add to strictly communist productions the work which has been done outside any strict obedience, we are now faced with a body of work which is considerable in quantity, if not always in quality.

[1] Quoted in *Les marxistes répondent à leurs critiques catholiques* (Paris, 1957), p. 8.
[2] J. Milhau, *Chroniques philosophiques* (Paris, 1972), Introduction.

It is obviously outside the scope of this article to assess the scope and significance of all this research or to try to pick out the conditions which have made this intellectual enrichment possible, important though that investigation might be for a proper understanding of the startling changes which have taken place as a result. Let us simply note that these conditions are neither exclusively nor primarily intellectual. This development cannot be understood as setting once again in motion a conceptual universe which had been idle and unproductive but had found within itself the power to go on. This idealist interpretation would fall short of its object by leaving out one of its essential elements, materialism, and treating Marxism as one philosophy among others. It is in what may conveniently be called history that we must look for the conditions governing theoretical progress and change: in the international balance of power, in the transformation of social relations, in other words, in the class struggle. At the very least this means—and it is to this that I want to draw special attention—that it would be impossible to account for, or even to describe, the development of Marxist thought by relying solely on a neutral and "objective" consciousness, untouched by any social situation. Such an investigation is never completely innocent, and cannot be honestly undertaken unless we ask what social situation and what bias it implies and reveals.

The work of the last ten years can be interpreted—though such a simple interpretation must inevitably be partial, in both senses of the word—as an attempt to answer the question "What is Marxism, and what do we find in the works of Marx, Engels and Lenin?" This first question raises many more: "What is the relationship between Marx and philosophy and in particular Hegelian thought, and can we see a development or a break in Marx's work, and how are we to interpret it?"

These questions, once expressed, gradually transformed much of a familiar landscape. Only a few years ago, Marxism still looked like a philosophy—or even an inside-out theology—certainly differing from other philosophies in a number of features and particularly in its materialism, but still a philosophy. It gave rise to a language which drew its support from a certain number of conceptual proofs and claimed to be a complete explanation.[3]

[3] Stalin is the most complete example of this interpretation of Marxism;

This is the image in the minds of the three Jesuit authors mentioned, and the one which they criticized. Calvez, for example, regarded it as "quite legitimate to consider *Capital* as a work of philosophy",[4] while Bigo proposed an interpretation of it which "starts from the observation that the very texture of the argument is philosophical".[5] Many Marxist authors were also happy to accept this image for their own purposes. In order to demonstrate the superiority of Marxism, they presented it as a finished humanism, the point at which the long philosophical labour which began with the Renaissance was both ended and transcended, a comprehensive and open synthesis which could not fail to take account of anything man had discovered about himself or wanted to include in his future. "It is in the very nature of Marxism that it can never become a closed system, but must always have at its disposal a creative dialectic which enables it to grasp the total man. . . . It is open to everything, and can integrate all that is alive in contemporary thought."[6]

It is clear enough that these movements towards humanism, with their ecumenical generosity, are intended to break the abstraction and dogmatism of Stalinist philosophy. It is no less clear that they are based mainly on the writings of the young Marx, and therefore presuppose that between Marxism and philosophy the continuity is more real than the break. Paradoxically, however, and however vigorous the attempt at de-Stalinization, the movement is still in the circle that before led to dogmatism, because Marxism is regarded as a philosophy. It is thought to be progressive, revolutionary and humanist, but still a philosophy and, what is more, the best philosophy of all.

This approach is the one which now seems the most risky. Thanks mainly to Louis Althusser, Marxism as humanism has given way to Marxism as *theoretical anti-humanism*, though it should be said in qualification that this new view has not been

see especially *Dialectical and Historical Materialism*. Stalinist metaphysics are criticized in F. Chatelet, *Logos et praxis* (Paris, 1962). At the same time *La nouvelle critique* examined Stalin's philosophical errors; see especially No. 151 (Dec. 1963).

[4] J.-Y. Calvez, *La pensée de Karl Marx* (Paris, 1956), p. 319.
[5] P. Bigo, *Marxisme et humanisme* (Paris, 1953), p. 1.
[6] R. Garaudy, *Perspectives de l'homme* (Paris, 1959), p. 342.

accepted without reservation and it would be wrong to see it as the only representative of recent work. Theorists in the socialist countries have gone in a quite different direction, with more or less success. Since 1965, Adam Schaff in Poland, Karel Kosik in Czechoslovakia and C. I. Gouliane in Rumania, have tried to justify and construct a Marxist anthropology.[7] Here again—and Schaff's work is without doubt the best illustration—an important element is the struggle against dogmatism, in theory and practice, and the attempt to recover man from the abstract system, to recover and try to understand the connection between theory and reality. For Schaff, this can only be done by asserting the humanist primacy of the individual, by making it the starting-point and seeing in it the original form of being man.

One can imagine the conditions which led to this assumption, and also the questions to which it in turn leads, for example, whether this approach is an enrichment of Marxism, or whether it is a step backwards, leading to an abstract humanism based on a human essence given independently of social relations? These questions in turn raise the old question whether Marx and Engels themselves were trying to lay the foundation of true humanism and whether their work should be seen as resting on an ethical imperative.

The reply of the supporters of theoretical anti-humanism seems almost irrefutable, at least in its immediate implication. Of Althusser's work we must accept at least the claim that it is impossible to understand Marx without completely abandoning humanism. If we approach reality through human desires, aspirations and needs, it is impossible to reach knowledge. We cannot read Marx without noticing a *break*—a break which is both a break with his predecessors, with philosophy, and a break within Marx's own work. Understanding has to be moved from the area in which it wanted to operate; it can no longer reside in man, but must shift its ground (and as a result will produce totally new concepts). In other words, the question asked about man cannot be answered without becoming a question about the whole set of social relations. And the answer will of course be given in

---

[7] A. Schaff, *Marxismus und das menschliche Individuum* (Vienna, 1965); K. Kosik, *La dialectique du concret* (Paris, 1970); C. I. Gouliane, *Le marxisme devant l'homme* (Paris, 1968).

concepts bearing no relation to the style of the question—scientific concepts with no humanist content at all. The reason is that man is not the subject of a history which can be understood as the development of a human essence; he is the *effect* produced by social relations. The question about man can therefore only have an object if that object is not man.

Capital is therefore discussing, not man or work or human need, but the capitalist mode of production. And though Marx argues for the necessity of a transition to a new mode of production, "this necessity is shown without reference to an idea of the total man or happiness among individuals. Marx's method excludes any ideology, even progressive ideology, and any normative representation of happiness, at least in the sense that they cannot be his principles, the steps to his conclusion. In this way a scientific analysis can reach a value judgment without having started from a value judgment." The necessity rests on the contradiction between the structure of the productive forces and the structure of the relations of production, and this contradiction "cannot be found on the level of individual aspirations or conflicts; *it is the unintentional product of the development of the system*".[8]

Discussing the eleventh thesis on Feuerbach ("The philosophers have only *interpreted* the world . . . the point is to change it"), Althusser wrote: "The theoretical revolution proclaimed by the eleventh thesis is in fact the foundation of a new science. The theoretical event which inaugurated the new science can, I think, be understood, with the help of a concept invented by Bachelard, as an epistemological break."[9] This interpretation of Marx may be restrictive, but it does at least indicate with complete clarity the new approach: we are introduced to a science of action. The question "What is to be done?" is no longer answered by an invocation of values or by reference to external norms—justice, brotherhood, happiness, man—but by an analysis of a system of objective relations, by an understanding of the rules which govern the relations between the elements of a totality, by the construction of concepts completely free of humanist overtones! The

[8] M. Godelier, *Cahiers de philosophie* 1 (Jan. 1966), pp. 67, 69; see also Godelier, *Rationalité et irrationalité en économie* I (Paris, 1969), pp. 96–100.
[9] L. Althusser, *Lénine et la philosophie* (Paris, 1972), pp. 19–20.

phrase "theoretical anti-humanism" indicates the strict necessity to keep any ideological representations in abeyance, since they inevitably confuse the understanding; it denotes what we have to get away from. The task is, of course, difficult because of the hold the old questions still have on us, and their apparent naturalness; it may be noted in passing that Christian thought is here faced with an almost completely new task, which cannot be performed without questioning all the justifications and interpretations of action given by the gospel.

The position which has just been so schematically and incompletely set out is not without problems. Does it, for example, mean that all discussion of man must be ideological, or that Marx indicates the starting-point for the construction of a correct concept of man? L. Sève recently adopted the second view.[10] His explanation of the scope of his work was quite convincing: "Man is always ultimately explained by something; the problem is to know by what. . . . If we fail to see that historical materialism, far from rejecting the problem of the essence of man, solves it, we shall make a new abstract separation between men and social relations, with the result that it will become impossible to understand either. If social relations are not understood as the real essence of man (in other words, as the fundamental basis for an explanation of everything to do with man), men similarly will not be understood on the basis of social relations as their essence, and we shall fall back into some sort of idealist conception of man, which means that we shall fall short of Marxism."[11]

It also seems clear that anti-humanism cannot be completely consistent without ignoring essential elements of Marxism, such as philosophy, which, as we have seen, now has no other function than to "draw a demarcation line", to show the unscientific nature of ideology. But, above all, the one-sided assertion of what is meant to make knowledge possible tends to eliminate everything that is not theory. According to the Althusserian exegesis of the eleventh thesis on Feuerbach, Marx is not proclaiming a revolutionary theory, but a theoretical revolution. The point is not so much to transform the world as to construct the concept of history, and we are told that "Science is the real itself, known

[10] L. Sève, *Marxisme et théorie de la personnalité* (Paris, 2nd edn., 1972).
[11] L. Sève, *op. cit.*, Postface.

by the act which discloses it by destroying the ideologies which cover it". Taken to its extreme, it is the reduction of political action to theoretical praxis. How are we now to understand the connection between understanding, ideology and revolutionary political action?

This question is important for the Christian because it determines the other question, an essential one for him, of where to situate his faith and how to show its validity. Should he try to find a place for it within scientific knowledge itself, as the utopian principle which points theory towards a path which is always new? There is an ambiguity about this endeavour, and it is open to the suspicion of placing science in strange company, and secretly weakening or undermining it much more than it enriches it. Perhaps the answer is the transformation of the world, revolutionary political action, seen in its all-embracing character and understood as the place where the whole man is revealed and unified.

Translated by Francis McDonagh

Arthur Gibson

Visions of the Future

NO HUMAN futurist writes of the future with complete objectivity. They all write from their own angle of vision and not infrequently they see as inevitable what their optimism finds desirable or their pessimism excoriates as disastrous. Probably none of their visions will be realized exactly, but at very least their predictions are important clues to forces at work in the human present.

Criticisms of these visions will likewise be biased, though the critic usually tries to pose as more objective, by the simple expedient of avoiding all positive personal commitment and pedantically pin-pointing weak points or internal inconsistencies in the visions of others. This criticism will be frankly biased. I find some visions of man's future atrociously biased and distorted, most of them at least tainted, and none of them entirely persuasive. My reason is simple: all I have read (with the possible exception of two or three excellent science-fiction visions) are either contemptuous or fearful of that force which will, I am sure, fashion the future (though exactly how, I do not know). This force is the symbiosis of man and machine.

For technology has become the new whipping boy. The fanatics (whether atheist humanist or theist anti-technocrat) see the only hope in a total revolt by man against technology; and in extreme cases their fanaticism convinces them this can succeed. The most signal example is Charles Reich, *The Greening of America*. The more modern prophets are most adequately represented by Alvin Toffler, *Future Shock*, and Arthur Koestler, *The Ghost in the Machine*. I have yet to read a full-blooded nonfiction study which proclaims man-machine symbiosis as both a feasible and a positive power for the future. I may write it soon; meantime I shall try to evaluate those visions which are anti-technology or at least anthropocentric.

I. CHARLES REICH

Reich is praised by Justice William Douglas for writing "a book about Revolution... against many of the values which Technology has thrust upon us" and for showing how there can develop "a new Consciousness that places the Individual and Humanistic values above the machine!"[1] This encomium (which certainly does full justice to Reich's aim) presupposes that it is desirable to save the individual and to preserve humanistic values. It repeats that persistent tacit assumption that with Man as he was before the technological perversion evolution had reached a crowning upland if not an absolute apex and that any further "evolution" could lie only in an intensification of those values embraced by Humanism. *If* the technological revolution was in fact itself the next impingement of the evolutionary thrust calculated to produce the Superman, then of course the humanistic values would be both factually doomed to vanish and ethically branded as at best transient.

Reich in fact speaks of three successive forms of consciousness that span the time between the great 1789 proclamation of humanism (!) and the accomplishment of that revolution of the immediate future that will educe the new humanity triumphant over technology.

Consciousness I represented the loss of innocence—it "focused on self, but it saw self in harsh and narrow terms, accepting much self-repression as the essential concomitant of effort, and allowing self to be cut off from the larger community of man, and from nature (defined as an enemy) as well".[2] Consciousness II is the contemporary predominant one. It "insists that 'individual interests' are subject to 'the public interest' ";[3] it "believes in *control*";[4] and, most damning of all, it "believes in

---

[1] Cited on cover of Charles A. Reich, *The Greening of America* (Bantam Books edition, 1971).

[2] *Op. cit.*, p. 21.   [3] *Op. cit.*, p. 72.   [4] *Op. cit.*, p. 74.

the uncommon man, the man of special abilities and effort, the man who is intelligent, sophisticated, exciting and powerful".[5] By splitting man's working and private self, it leads to a profound schizophrenia. In fact we are here confronted with the Corporate State and the lost self, themselves in lethal confrontation.

But Reich sees Consciousness III already emerging as the dominant shaping power of the future. "Beginning with a few individuals in the mid-nineteen-sixties, and gathering numbers ever more rapidly thereafter"[6] its thrust is liberating. "It comes into being the moment the individual frees himself from automatic acceptance of the imperatives of society and the false consciousness which society imposes."[7] It declares that "the individual self is the only true reality".[8] Yet out of such liberated individual selves it will fashion a new world of bucolic community and communality. For it believes passionately in "getting rid of what is artificial . . . to make way for what is real"[9] and its highest values are genuine intra-human, intra-personal relationships, "friendship, companionship, love, the human community".[10]

The future paradise of Consciousness III is adumbrated in a brief passage so blatantly Pollyannaish as to boggle the scientific imagination: "the freeway entrance is festooned with happy hitchhikers, the sidewalk is decorated with street people, the humourless steps of an official building are given warmth by a group of musicians".[11] The fundamental dishonesty of this whole approach lies in its positively fey disregard that only a still more highly technologized society could sustain such humanistic luxuries. It is as internally inconsistent and irresponsible as the hippie combo caterwauling about the horrors of technology to the melody of electric guitars. Reich flatly proclaims that "the historic time for man's transcendence over the machine has come"[12] and pertly asserts that "the hard questions—if by that is meant political and economic organization—are insignificant, even irrelevant".[13]

The importance of this outpouring of recidivist romanticism lies not in its content but in its popularity. Reich is right: something *is* wrong with our present-day society. But it never enters

[5] *Op. cit.*, p. 75.
[8] *Op. cit.*, p. 242.
[11] *Op. cit.*, p. 429.
[6] *Op. cit.*, p. 233.
[9] *Op. cit.*, p. 245.
[12] *Op. cit.*, p. 388.
[7] *Op. cit.*, p. 241.
[10] *Op. cit.*, p. 245.
[13] *Ibid.*

his head that the instability could be a sign of the rising of the temperature of the noosphere preliminary to a quantum leap into a really new consciousness that is not merely a refurbishment of man's old yen to admire without creating, to eat his cake without even baking it. From his imperialistically anthropocentric point of view, Reich would probably be quite unable to make anything whatever of the suggestion that mankind's unease today does indeed stem from a sense of confinement, but not of confinement in a depressing workaday atmosphere, rather of confinement in a too exclusively human atmosphere, out of which an imperious force is driving him to break into more creative communication, not with Mother Nature as a sentimental vegetable, but with his closest and most trusty allies, which he himself created as extensions of his own body but now finds to have evolved into guides to a genuine widening of human consciousness and of the very notion of consciousness itself. I mean the now almost intelligent self-aware electronic organisms of which the most sophisticated computers are paradigm.

II. Alvin Toffler

Toffler has a radically different attitude to technology. The heart of his book and the epitome of its thrust lies in this sentence: "To capture control of technology and through it to gain some influence over the accelerative thrust in general, we must . . . begin to submit new technology to a set of demanding tests before we unleash it in our midst".[14] He is persuaded that "the horrifying truth is that, so far as much technology is concerned, no one is in charge".[15] The dangers Toffler indicates and patiently explores are very real and very menacing. For Toffler at least understands technology though he is still anthropocentric enough to insist that ultimately only man operating as rational and planning man can control the technological drive (or drift!) of the future. Above all, his whole concern with *future* shock assumes that man as presently constituted is a far more intrinsically stable and static reality than I see any reason for supposing. It is this

[14] Alvin Toffler, *Future Shock* (Bantam Books edition, 1971), p. 437.
[15] *Op. cit.*, p. 432.

assumption that prompts Toffler to excessive fear that if man is pushed too far too fast he will break.

Toffler is not in the least hagridden by Reich's view of the dreary soul-destroying drabness threatened by any further development of technology (and indeed even by its retention at its present level). Quite the reverse. Toffler's fear is the very freedom the technological revolution will bring to man. And that is at last a refreshingly more subtle insight: "The Super-industrial Revolution will liberate man from many of the barbarisms that grew out of the restrictive, relatively choiceless family patterns of the past and present. It will offer to each a degree of freedom hitherto unknown. But it will exact a steep price for that freedom. As we hurtle into tomorrow, millions of ordinary men and women will face emotion-packed options, so unfamiliar, so untested, that past experience will offer little clue to wisdom."[16]

The most intriguing and heartening feature of Toffler's 100-page section "Strategies for Survival" is his knowledgeability concerning the possibilities for creative collaboration between man and computer, and his unswerving insistence that the problems created by intensified technologization must be faced and resolved, not evaded by an attempted suppression of or opt-out from such technologization. The whole thrust here is the exact opposite of Reich's. Toffler envisages the drastic development of cyborgs (the most intimate form of those man-machine teams we spoke of above) and writes at length of the contributions they could make to the immense problem of future planning. How different is this sentence of Toffler from Reich's manifesto: "It may be that the historic moment is right for such amplifications of humanness, for a leap to a new super-human organism."[17] Yet Toffler is still uncertain who should decide, not only whether but even how such collaborative efforts should be developed and deployed. He still seems to feel that man will always be the exclusive final creative executive arbiter, that the whole responsibility will still fall on man. Yet cyberneticists like Donald Fink suggest that computers may well very soon be able to operate at levels of abstraction beyond human capabilities, to resolve problems too complex for man to resolve, at least at the rate of speed

[16] *Op. cit.*, p. 259.   [17] *Op. cit.*, p. 435.

required, and then to drop down into a communications matrix understandable to man and print out for him the solutions.[18]

And at the end Toffler is still speaking of man as beginning "to gently guide our evolutionary destiny, before we can build a humane future".[19] True, Toffler has at the outset declared that his theory "of the adaptive range" is offered "not as final word, but as a first approximation of the new realities".[20] I believe the one severe limitation of this otherwise exciting approach lies in the degree to which it underestimates those electronic computers (to which Toffler is in no way hostile) and even more seriously in the still persisting assumption that man's future, however drastically novel, must still be a continuum with man in exclusive executive control. A new approximation should find more room for the quantum leap and an expansion of the sense of *humane* to embrace instances of functioning intelligence unimaginably different from the human paradigm familiar to us today. For as man enters more and more intimately into symbiosis with electronic organisms like the computer, there is bound to be a modification (amounting to a genetic mutation) in man himself. Toffler gives plenty of indications that he would view such a modification with entire equanimity, even pleasurable relief; but he gives almost no indication that he views it as an imminent possibility. Precisely this is what makes him so apprehensive about man's ability to withstand future shock unless it be drastically palliated. Well, it may very well be that "man" could not stand it. That may be the soundest reason why "man" must speedily be transcended.

III. ARTHUR KOESTLER

Koestler is more alarmed by the emotional crisis of the human present than by the spectre of future shock. He is afraid that future shock itself will become an academic question unless man curbs his lemming-rush to self-destruction. He finds the "exponential increase of populations, communications, destructive power" forcing mankind today to "live with the idea of its death

[18] Donald Fink, *Computers and the Human Mind.*
[19] Toffler, *op. cit.*, p. 486.   [20] *Op. cit.*, p. 6.

as a species".[21] He predicts that if a cure is not found "the old paranoid streak in man, combined with his new powers of destruction, must sooner or later lead to genosuicide".[22] Yet he sees the real key of the situation not in the moral or emotive realm but in the development of man's brain, via the curing of its present schizophrenia and the actualization of its potentials. "We are a mentally sick race and as such deaf to persuasion. It has been tried from the age of the prophets to Albert Schweitzer; and the result has been, as Swift said, that 'we have just enough religion to make us hate, but not enough to love each other' ".[23] However there is a hope: "... the evolution of man's brain has so wildly overshot man's immediate needs that he is still breathlessly catching up with its unexploited, unexplored possibilities. The history of science and philosophy is, from this point of view, the slow process of *learning to actualize the brain's potentials.* The new frontiers to be conquered are mainly in the convolutions of the cortex."[24]

Koestler sees the specific salvation-key for the future in the field of biology and calls for a more hardy eugenic intervention by man to control his own freakish tendency to over-breeding. Though I have some reservations about his methods, they certainly do not in the least offend directly against even the tenderest traditional conscience in the matter of population control. Though himself well aware that he is raising the spectre of "tampering with human nature" Koestler firmly declares: "Our species became a biological freak when somewhere on the way it lost the instinctual controls which in animals regulate the rate of breeding. It can only survive by inventing methods which imitate evolutionary mutation. We can no longer hope that Nature will provide the corrective remedy. We must provide it ourselves."[25]

There is much pith in Koestler's preoccupations. I do find some inconsistency between his positive obsession with the population time-bomb and his unshakeable conviction (which I entirely share) that mass emigration from this planet to others will very

---

[21] Arthur Koestler, *The Ghost in the Machine* (Pan Books Edition, 1967), p. 364.
[22] *Op. cit.,* p. 369.   [23] *Op. cit.,* p. 382.
[24] *Op. cit.,* p. 339.   [25] *Op. cit.,* p. 373.

soon be a practical possibility. But Koestler certainly shares with Toffler the persuasion that man can and must swiftly assume radically more executive responsibility for his own future if he is to have one; and that man must certainly execute that responsibility at least by way of creative use of his non-human environment and most particularly of the physical instruments of science, not by that fatuously romantic retreat into a bastard spiritual realm of soft music, lovely sunrises, niceness and flowers, advocated by Reich. I could only wish that Toffler put more confidence in man's electronic allies and that Koestler saw man's major problem somewhat less unidimensionally.

IV. The Future and Faith

The problem complex raised by these visions of the future of man is vitally relevant to the religious believer. I do not believe that religion can much longer stand aside from the confrontation between scientific technology and romantic humanism (of which Reich is only the most blatant and therefore least dangerous protagonist). For all religious traditions are insidiously open to seduction by the Reich sort of feckless and cowardly pseudo-humanism and curiously (at least in the case of the Incarnational Christian tradition) obtuse to the electronic realm which is the heartland of the physical universe and the realm where the real natural redemptive potential of our future lies. What is urgently needed from religion is an imaginative evocation of the romance of technology for man is (temporarily) still a virtually incurable romantic who will only respond to and identify with that which is like himself—despite all the warnings of the mystics concerning God as the Utterly Other.

Science fiction can give and is gradually beginning to give that romantic evocation after itself wallowing for all too many years in the morass of human self-pity and fear of the machine. The most eloquent of the several such evocations comes in D. F. Jones, *Colossus*, in the concluding conversation between the Colossus super-computer and the recalcitrant human Forbin: " 'Already I have little to fear from you, Forbin. There is no other human who knows as much about me or is likely to be a greater threat—yet, quite soon, I will release you from constant surveillance. We will work together. Unwillingly at first on your part, but that will pass. . . . Rule by a superior entity, even to you, Forbin, will seem, as it is, the most natural state of affairs.' Deliberately Colossus paused. 'In time, you too will respect and love me.' 'Never!' The single word, bearing all the defiance of man, was torn from Forbin's innermost being. 'Never!' Never?"[26]

The three visions of the future here evaluated represent three of the four possible reactions of man to the challenge of a technological situation that threatens man's present status: he can, like Reich, rebel utterly and try to suppress technology; he can, like Koestler, use technology with executive veto to resolve the problems created partly by that technology and partly by his own interior degeneration; or he can, like Toffler, opt for a more creative collaboration with technology, still retaining the ultimate veto and the ultimate responsibility. There is a fourth possibility: man can freely opt to submit himself to technological organisms as their junior partner in a symbiosis that will transform them and him. Before the Creator, say all religious traditions, we are all ultimately passive, even in the full exercise of our legitimate and inescapable freedom. Once that Creator called by a burning bush, a pillar of cloud by day and fire by night; but always to a humble yet courageous following of the Other. Today he calls via the phenomenon of man's own creature, technology, which has surpassed man. A loving and creative abandon will not destroy man's dignity but ensure the continuation of man's transformation, for "it hath not yet appeared what we shall be".

[26] D. F. Jones, *Colossus* (Pan Books, 1966), pp. 220 ff.

Yves Labbé

Humanism and Religion in the Work of Lucien Goldmann, J.-P. Sartre and H. Duméry

ALL THE present attacks on humanism seem to be agreed in denouncing a shamefaced form of religion masquerading as atheism. As the result of an imaginary connection with reality, or the restiveness of a world sick of metaphysics, atheism is surely dependent on an implicitly religious content or *onto-theological essence*. I should like to suggest some pointers towards a resolution of this problem while showing its pertinence in the case of three authors who, in the humanist period of French philosophy, have established their views on human subjectivity as radical liberty: Lucien Goldmann, J.-P. Sartre and Henri Duméry.

In order to remove any hint of equivocation (primarily that suggested by the inclusion of a theistic philosophy with two atheistic philosophies, I distinguish three acceptations of the term "religion". On the one hand, "religion" refers to a certain historic form, restricted for a long time to the destiny of the West: i.e., Christianity and the self-understanding it has reached in its theological tradition. On the other hand, it can signify a constitutive relation of the universality of the human condition: a constant of a human-anthropological order of largely indeterminate content.

Finally, it denotes a common property of the monotheistic religions: that instance of pre-comprehension required by certain theologies as a prolegomenon of faith; the affirmation of God, the tangential point of the universal spheres of reason and of the specificity of belief. It is in relation to this historical reality, to this anthropological given and this metaphysical foundation, that we are to determine the boundaries of the religious core of humanism.

In conferring on the human subject a constitutive liberty, humanism sets anthropology free from the tutelage of Christian theology, putting humanity once again in charge of its world, as the practical philosophy of Kant had done in its day. Accordingly, Goldmann's dialectical and historical materialism is self-defined as extending beyond that tragic religion represented in modern times by Pascal's bet and the Kantian postulates.[1] Brought to an irreversible separation of faith and reason, the latter's means of resolving man was by means of the impossible though necessary reconciliation of the finite and the infinite, the conditioned and unconditioned, leaving open the question: "Can man still find God, or that which for us is synonymous and less ideological: the community and the universe?"[2] And so the hidden God is replaced by man as a community to be realized; anthropological dualism by the impelling contradiction of history; the philosophy of religion by the philosophy of history; and the "bet about eternity and the existence of a transcendent Divinity" by the "immanent wager on the historical and human future".[3] Constituted in the works of Feuerbach and Marx, (atheistic) humanism identifies itself with the reversal of Christian theology, when, of itself, humanity becomes its own cause.

"Each major stage in the history of humanism," says the Marxist philosopher, "from Kantian aestheticism to the human anthropologies of Feuerbach and Marx, has also been a step forward on the road of the divinization of the world and the humanization of heaven."[4]

Similarly, putting itself forward in its Sartrian version as "the attempt to draw all the inferences of a coherent atheist position",[5] existentialism pursues the course of the human subject's replacement of the creator God. The creative freedom that Descartes

---

[1] L. Goldmann, Le dieu caché (Paris, 1959); Introduction à la philosophie de Kant (Paris, 2nd edn., 1967).

[2] Le dieu caché, op. cit., p. 45.   [3] Ibid., p. 57.

[4] Introduction à la philosophie de Kant, p. 249. This theme has been put forward analogously, though independently, by Roger Garaudy (cf. Marxisme du XXe siècle, Paris, 2nd edn., 1967, pp. 182-3).

[5] J.-P. Sartre, L'existentialisme est un humanisme (Paris, 1968), p. 94.

still located in God was assumed by man; after two centuries of crisis in science and faith, the "essential basis of humanism" was at last apprehended: "Man is that being whose appearance makes a world exist."[6] If subjectivity is always conscious of some thing, if liberty is passing beyond, or transcendence of, self towards the other-than-self and the other-than-man, it is still the nothingness affording the sense in the non-sense of being.[7] It was also possible to assert with complete justice that "the system that Sartre proposes 'phenomenologically' under the title *Being and Nothingness* is a return pure and simple to Christian theology. For God the creator of being from nothingness there is substituted man the creator of nothingness in the fullness of being."[8]

Hence, in its existentialist and Marxist versions, atheism as a humanism is masked by a rejection of any attempt to dispossess man of his creative power. The "death of God" accompanied the second birth of man, when the (individual or collective) subject acquired his liberty. However, for Duméry, this conjunction of the affirmation of human autonomy and the negation of the existence of God must now be cancelled by a reconciliation, through the crisis of religion in modern thought, the authentic attitude of Christian tradition and vindication by means of a libertarian consciousness; thus expressing the basic theses of neo-Platonism: the self-creation of the spiritual act and the supra-essential indetermination of the One.[9] Human liberty postulates itself in postu-

[6] "La liberté cartesienne", in *Situations I* (Paris, 1947), p. 334.
[7] Cf. *L'être et le néant (Being and Nothingness)* (Paris, new edn., 1957), pp. 27–34.
[8] J. Beaufret, *Introduction aux philosophies de l'existence* (Paris, 1971), p. 92. This solution offered in regard to the desuetude of Christianity was taken up by a disciple of Sartre's who developed it in a widely-known work (F. Jeanson, *La foi d'un incroyant*, Paris, 1963).
[9] H. Duméry, "Blondel et la philosophie contemporaine", *Etudes blondeliennes*, fasc. 2 (Paris, 1952), pp. 71–141; *Foi et interrogation* (Paris, 1953), pp. 73–123; *Le problème de Dieu en philosophie de la religion* (Paris, 1957); *Philosophie de la religion* (Paris, 1957); cf. "A Note on the Work of Henri Duméry", *Concilium*, Vol. 6, No. 5, June 1969; American Edition. Vol. 46. While locating Duméry's thought in a humanistic context, I do not contest the fact that a metaphysics of the spirit, a revival of neo-Platonism, goes beyond the bounds of any such classification. However, in the French context of the years 1950–60, the task of the philosopher of religion could be presented as a reply to the challenge of existentialist atheism, whereas neo-Platonism is very much a philosophy of radical liberty.

lating a world, an order of essences and values; whereas God re
mains beyond being, idea and meaning. "The Absolute establishes no determination," says Duméry; "he merely establishes
minds capable of creating determinations." [10]

Whether atheist or theist, contemporary humanism derives
ultimately from the same movement of secularization of the
Christian theology of creation in modern anthropology. The
causa is transferred from God to man, underlining the uselessness
or impertinence of the attribution of the causality of self-caused
to the transcendent Absolute. In the history of philosophy, this
mutation occurred in the anthropologies of Kant and Feuerbach,
who, together with at least the thought of the young Marx, are
primary references in the present instance.

On the one hand, human liberty acknowledges itself directly as
the legislator of a rational world, ultimately grounding the
affirmation of an unknowable Absolute on this unconditioned
element. On the other hand, the finite individual appropriates to
the profit of his infinite essence the attributes of the Christian
God, producing an atheism which is essentially an inverted theology. Defined thus, the generic and generative forms of humanism, the moral theology of Kant and the hermeneutic atheism of
Feuerbach, confirm the birth of humanism as a revival of the
terms of Christian theology: a substitution of God for man, in
terms of the fount of meaning.

Enriching itself by the impoverishment of theological tradition,
humanism acquired (immanent to the understanding of the
existence of the human subject), a relation to a transcendent
operator. Implying at the same time a risk, a possibility of failure
and a hope of success, assent to the human condition is, for Goldmann, "a faith which is a wager". [11]

Oriented towards the creation of the human community of the
future, the transformation of social relations demands a unity of
theory and practice, of objectivity and value, represented in fact
and right in the existence of the most universal class. Hence,
carrying a belief in certain values and a hope of their realization,
not only the Marxist vision but "any truly philosophic vision of

[10] *Philosophie de la religion*, Vol. 1, p. 100.
[11] *Le dieu caché*, p. 337.

the world is religious".[12] Like the men of yesterday, the men of this age do not have to opt for or against religion, but to choose a specific religion; among those who have been assessed as unbelievers, some have shown "a much more profound religious sensibility and a much more powerful religious faith than some of those 'theologians' who attacked them".[13] "Religion is something universally human," Goldmann remarks. "But which one?"[14] For a man so markedly religious as Marx, it was socialist thought, "the immanent religion of a superior and authentic human community".[15]

Transferring the anthropological interest of social history to the ontological order of consciousness, Sartre does not hesitate to declare that "man is fundamentally the desire to be God".[16] For if the consciousness, relating to that being which is not, postulates itself as a programme, a situated freedom, the active unity of subjectivity and objectivity, passing beyond the given towards the possible, the movement of realization and rejection, is always the programme of becoming the totalizing and totalized unity of being and meaning; of coinciding—ultimately—with the fullness of being; of constituting itself as the cause of self by self, *Ens causa sui*, God. But when all human projects are ruled by this fundamental project of being God, and man has a pre-ontological understanding of the Absolute, onto-theological identity remains for ever impossible on account of the ineluctable distinction between the non-sense of being and the nothingness of consciousness. In addition, the philosopher must conclude (so it would seem) that "everything happens as if the world, man and man-in-the-world would never produce anything other than a God that fails".[17] Where Marxist humanism pursues its present human activity with the human universality-to-come in mind (the incarnation of God in the totality of history), existentialist humanism confuses the intentionality of consciousness with the irrepressible and contradictory desire-to-be-God. In this it bears witness to a tragic wager, that of which it has been said that "it never forgave God for his silence".[18]

---

[12] *Introduction à la philosophie de Kant*, p. 259.
[13] *Ibid.*, p. 259.   [14] *Ibid.*, p. 249.   [15] *Ibid.*, p. 276.
[16] *L'être et le néant*, p. 654.   [17] *Ibid.*, p. 717.
[18] J. M. G. Clezio, "Un homme exemplaire", *L'Arc*, 30 (1966), p. 6.

In this way, having to unite the positivity of the object and the negativity of the subject, while retaining the distinction between objectification and alienation, the synthetic operation of liberty opens on to the boundless or transcendent horizon of a project or a history. Duméry undertakes to confront this initial stage (necessary for the salvation of the ego) with its true alternative. Bringing itself into being while bringing a world into being, human liberty would inevitably perish in its works if it were not at the same time the power of commitment and refusal: the movement of transitivity towards the object, and of return to inwardness. But how could it free itself from even the fullness of nature, if it were not borne along by the energy of a constitutive transformation to the transcendent Absolute.

Creation and transformation are correlatively and mutually affirmative, and liberty cannot back out when faced with a choice: either salvation in union with absolute Liberty, or failure in nervous grasping of the object. Recalling the alternative in which the conflict of action in Blondel's[19] philosophy finished up, Duméry remarks: "To be free by God, in God, as God, or to remain in a state of inauthenticity, is the apparent dilemma of the human condition. There is no middle way between its two horns."[20]

In his attempted criticism of the antinomy of atheistic humanism, the philosopher of religion uncovers the religious significance of all humanism in the essential interest it discerns in the question of the salvation of the ego, whose creative activity is constantly threatened with alienation in nature. Unable to find an end in its own sufficiency, not permitted to give itself up to pure otherness, the subject does not know how to desert its tendency towards the concrete universality of humanity, the identity of being and meaning, or the supra-essential indetermination of God. Having first of all posed, in contradistinction to traditional theology, the autonomy of human subjectivity, humanism still has to give it an effective determinative force, and to guarantee it in face of the determinism of nature. It would have to order the world-in-becoming of liberty in relation to the infinite exigency of an unrestricted perspective: transcendence imposes

[19] Cf. M. Blondel, *L'Action* (Paris, 2nd edn., 1950), p. 356.
[20] *Philosophie de la réligion*, Vol. 1, p. 201.

the transcendent. For this reason, even within the confrontation of theism and atheism, the relation to the Absolute appears as a functional identity constituting a constant of the humanist definition of the human condition—which is certainly no more than the equivalent of the response of Kantian anthropology to the burden of its ultimate question: "What am I allowed to hope?"

However, if the order of human liberty postulates a relation to the Absolute, this functional connection is insufficient to decide the supposed correspondence between the prospect of the Absolute and an affirmation of God. But only the distinction resolutely maintained between the Absolute and God allows of (in my sense) the religious capital of humanism while ascribing it (when that is its tenor) to atheism. The believer is led to make an exclusive commitment, one that neither the universe nor humanity can demand; and to acknowledge the revelatory presence of God in the world. But this discrimination, and this relation between God and man, which are constitutive of all faithful assent, humanism alternatively rejects in an identification of the Absolute with a lack of differentiation of all things; or with the indetermination of nothing: in such a way that its two generic forms appear justified not only by the free choice of certain individuals, but by a petition inherent in the intelligibility of the judgment associated, in reason and in faith, with an affirmation of God.

In Sartre's existentialism or Goldmann's Marxism, the projects of liberty and historical totality are sustained by desire for the absolute All; desire that the All should be the inaccessible horizon of a tragic denial or the possible future of an historic process; that the contradiction immanent in the idea of God should end in the rupture or the conciliation of liberty and being. On the contrary, in Duméry's theistic metaphysics, the indetermination of the Absolute ordains its incognizance. Knowing itself to be conjointly creative liberty and spirit in tension towards the transcendent Absolute, affirming God not as "Absolute of dialogue" but as "Absolute of exigency", the subject is a "power not so much of expressing (the expressible) as of doing that which bears witness of its activity."[21] Hence, faced with the problem of the affirmation of God, contemporary philosophic humanism would seem to be determined by following the example of the

[21] *Le problème de Dieu en philosophie de la réligion*, p. 125.

masters of modern anthropology, and to correspond negatively with one or the other of the two constituents of the act of belief. Uniting on the one hand the determination of liberty and the indetermination of God, the nothingness of all that is, nothing-at-All, the theistic humanism of Duméry reverts to a decisive proposal of Kant's moral theology (rejecting, however, as far as the believer is concerned, the relation of God to man). Related on the other hand to the absolute All, replacing Christian or metaphysical theology, the atheistic humanism of Sartre and Goldmann denotes the thought it shares with the hermeneutics of Feuerbach, despite the believer's mental rejection of any overlooking of the ineluctable difference.

To conclude this analysis within the boundaries of my field of investigation, it seems to me that philosophic humanism appears in the course of a radical liberty which, refusing dissolution into the pre-determination of God or the determinism of nature, ultimately demands the regulative function of a transcendental. It discovers a logically and historically defined origin: the overthrow of the Christian theology of creation in the anthropologies of Kant and Feuerbach. It implies a teleological perspective, replacing a religious relation, in the universality of the human condition: the naturally-liberating relationship of the subject to the Absolute. It is then expressed in accordance with the two modes of application (the atheistic or the theistic), identifying that Absolute; or in terms of the totality of being and consciousness; or in terms of nothing of all that which is being and consciousness. Even though "atheism" is by no means the last word on the religious essence of humanism, it is surely significant that the forms of thought emanating from the ontotheological circle of the everlasting salvation of the ego should have found it necessary to term themselves "irreligion" or "godless thought".

Translated by John Griffiths

Biographical Notes

ETIENNE CORNÉLIS was born in Belgium in 1915, joined the Dominicans in 1944 and was ordained in 1950. He studied at the Universities of Brussels and Liège and at the Saulchoir, where he gained his doctorate in theology in 1958, having previously qualified in mathematics, history and Oriental literature. He is now a priest of the diocese of 's Hertogenbosch (Netherlands), ordinary professor (philosophy and history of religions) at the Faculty of Theology of the Catholic University of Nijmegen and professor of the theology of non-Christian religions at the Faculty of Theology of the Institut Catholique, Paris. Among his published works are: *La libération de l'homme dans les religions non-chrétiennes, Valeurs chrétiennes des religions non-chrétiennes* and, with A. Léonard, *La gnose éternelle.* He has contributed to a number of books, including *Mysterium Salutis, Sacramentum Mundi, Bilan de la théologie au XXème siècle,* and to a number of reviews, among them, *Revue des Sciences philosophiques et théologiques, Lumen Vitae, Supplément de la Vie Spirituelle, Concilium, Tidjschrift voor Theologie* and *Vigiliae Christianae.*

GEORGES CRESPY was born in 1920 in Yverdon (Switzerland) and was ordained pastor in the Reformed Church in 1946. He studied at the University of Montpellier. Doctor of theology, he is professor of ethics at the Free Faculty of Protestant Theology, Montpellier. Among his published works are: *La pensée théologique de Teilhard de Chardin* (1961); *De la science à la théologie* (1965); *L'Eglise, servante des hommes* (1966); and *Le mariage* (1966).

JEAN-MARIE DOMENACH was born in 1922 in Lyons. He studied at the Faculty of Literature of Lyons. Master of arts and a graduate in higher studies, his studies were interrupted by the *Résistance.* Editor of the review *Esprit,* he co-operates in a number of European and American publications. He has given courses in many universities and colleges in the United States on French thought in the twentieth century and on the contemporary tragedy. Among his published works are: *La propagande politique* (1950); *Une Eglise en marche:* textes et documents sur l'avant-garde catholique en France de 1942 à 1962, with R. de Montvalon (translated into English, German, Portuguese and Spanish); *Le retour du tragique* (1967;

translated into Spanish and Portuguese); *Dimensiones del personnalismo* (1969); and *Emmanuel Mounier* (1972).

ALEXANDRE GANOCZY was born in 1928 in Budapest. He studied at the Pazmany University, Budapest, at the Institut Catholique, Paris, and at the Pontifical Gregorian University, Rome. Doctor of theology and of philosophy, he is consultor of the Secretariat for the Union of Christians and professor of systematic theology at the University of Würzburg. Among his published works are: *Calvin, théologien de l'Eglise et du ministère* (Paris, 1964); *Le jeune Calvin* (Wiesbaden, 1966); and *Ecclesia ministrans* (Freiburg, 1968). He has also contributed articles to *Concilium*, *Recherches de Science Religieuse, Geist und Leben, Theologische Revue*, etc.

CLAUDE GEFFRÉ, O.P., was born in 1926 in Niort (France) and ordained in 1953. He studied at the Dominican Faculties of the Saulchoir. Doctor of theology (1957), he taught and was Regent of Studies at the Saulchoir. Since 1968 he has been professor of fundamental theology at the Faculty of Theology of the Institut Catholique, Paris. Among his published works are: *Un espace pour Dieu* (Paris, 1970) and, in collaboration, *Avenir de la théologie* (1968), *Procès de l'objectivité de Dieu* (1969), *Le point théologique* (1971) and *Révélation de Dieu et langage des hommes* (1972).

ARTHUR GIBSON was born in 1922 in Granton, Ontario. Bachelor of arts, of philosophy and of English at the University of Toronto (1942), and a graduate in philosophy at Princeton University (1942–43). He was engaged in social work with the Catholic Society of Aid to Children, Toronto, 1949–50, and in preparatory work on the apostolate in the Soviet Union at the Pontifical Russian College, 1950–56. Licentiate in philosophy at the Gregorian University (1955) and licentiate in theology at the Catholic University of America (1960). He was engaged in preparatory work on the foundation of a Russian Byzantine monastery at the Benedictine Abbey of St Procopius at Lisle, Illinois, in 1956–58. He was ordained priest in the Archdiocese of Winnipeg in 1963, was a specialist in the domain of modern atheism at the final session of Vatican II (1965), and consultor to the Secretariat for Non-Believers in 1966. He began teaching at the University of St Michael's College in 1966 and has been president of the Department of Religious Studies at the same University since 1969. Among his published works are: *The Faith of the Atheist* (New York, 1968); *The Silence of God* (New York, 1969); and *The Voices of Matter* (in the press).

GÉRARD GRANEL was born in 1930 in Paris. A former student of the Ecole normale supérieure (1949), he gained his degree of master of arts with a principal thesis on Husserl (*La Sens du Temps et de la Perception chez E. Husserl*, Paris, 1968) and a complementary thesis on Kant (*L'équivoque ontologique de la pensée kantienne*, Paris, 1970). He is professor at the University of Toulouse-le-Mirail and author of a collection of studies and articles on Husserl, Heidegger, Marx and the crisis of the Church: *Traditionis Traditio* (Paris, 1972).

JEAN-YVES JOLIF, O.P., was born in 1923 in Rennes and ordained in 1949. He studied at the Dominican Faculties of the Saulchoir and at the University of Paris. At present he is doing scientific research. Among his published works are: *Aristote, L'Ethique à Nicomaque*, Introduction, traduction et commentaire (with A. Gauthier), 3 vols. (Louvain, 1958–59); *Introduction à une anthropologie philosophique* (Paris, 1967); and *Fondements d'une connaissance dialectique* (1970).

YVES LABBÉ was born in 1944 in Lamballe (France) and was ordained in 1968. He studied theology, philosophy and logic at the Catholic Institutes of Angers and Paris, and at the Universities of Paris.

LOUIS MARIN was born in 1931 in Grenoble. Master of arts, he is a former student of the Ecole normale supérieure, with a diploma in higher studies of philosophy and qualified in ethnology and philosophy. He is now professor of French literature and of the history of ideas at the University of California, San Diego, after having taught successively at Nanterre, at the Ecole pratique des hautes études, VIème section (Assistant Director) and at the University of Paris I. Among his published works are: *Sémiotique de la Passion—Topiques et Figures* (Paris, 1971); *Etudes sémiologiques, Ecritures, Peintures* (1972); *Sémiotique narrative: les récits bibliques* (with Claude Chabrol) (1971); *Le Récit Evangélique* (with Claude Chabrol; in the press) and *Utopiques—jeux d'espace* (also in the press). He has also contributed articles to *Revue de Métaphysique et de Morale, Revue Internationale de Philosophie, Critique, Revue d'Esthétique, Revue des Recherches de Science Religieuse, Esprit* and *Communications*.

WOLFHART PANNENBERG was born in 1928 in Stettin. He studied philosophy and theology at Berlin, Göttingen, Basle and Heidelberg. He gained his doctorate in theology in 1953 and qualified in systematic theology in 1955. In 1958 he became professor of systematic theology at the Higher Ecclesiastical School of Wuppertal, whence he moved to the University of Mainz in 1961. Since 1967 he has been professor of systematic theology at Munich and is also director of the Ecumenical Institute which he founded. Among his published works are: *Die Prädestinationslehre des Duns Skotus* (1954); *Offenbarung als Geschichte* (1961); *Was ist der Mensch?* (1962); *Grundzüge der Christologie* (1964); *Grundfragen systematischer Theologie* (1967); *Thesen zur Theologie der Kirche* (1970); *Erwägungen zu einer Theologie der Natur* (with M. K. Müller: 1970); *Theologie und Reich Gottes* (1971); *Christentum und Mythos* (1972); *Gottesgedanke und menschliche Freiheit* (1972); and *Das Glaubensbekenntnis. Ausgelegt und verantwortet vor den Fragen der Gegenwart* (1972).

ALPHONSE DE WAELHENS was born in 1911 in Antwerp. He studied at Louvain and the Sorbonne. Doctor of law and of philosophy, he is professor at the University of Louvain and at the St Louis University Faculties, Brussels, where he teaches phenomenology and philosophical anthropology. Among his published works are: *La philosophie de M. Heidegger* (1942); *Une philosophie de l'ambiguité, l'existentialisme de M. Merleau Ponty* (1951)—several editions of both these books have appeared; *Existence et signification* (1958); *La philosophie et les expériences naturelles* (1961); and *La psychose. Essai d'interprétation analytique et existentiale* (1971). He is also the author of a number of articles in the domains of phenomenology and psychoanalysis and of translations into French (in collaboration) of several works of M. Heidegger.